the treasury of
HORSES

the treasury of
HORSES

Contributors
Charles Chenevix Trench   Judith Campbell
Walter D Osborne   Michael Seth-Smith
Elwyn Hartley Edwards

Octopus Books

First published 1972 by
Octopus Books Limited
59 Grosvenor Street, London W 1

ISBN 7064 0019 4
© 1972 Octopus Books Limited

Produced by Mandarin Publishers Limited, Hong Kong
Printed in Hong Kong

Contents

6

The horse in Europe

CHARLES CHENEVIX TRENCH

The armour of a knight and his horse in the late fifteenth century. Such complicated and heavy pieces were developed as protection against the long bow, and rendered both man and horse very clumsy and slow in action.

Those whose pleasure it is to plumb the unfathomable depths of pre-history are generally agreed that the horse in Europe is descended from the 'tarpan' variety of wild horse, a smallish, mouse-grey animal with a black dorsal stripe, of which the last herd was exterminated in the Ukraine in 1851. It is just possible that there may have been a heavier breed of northern forest horse with a separate ancestry, and some Spanish authors claim for their country a distinct breed of wild horse; but most archaeologists and zoologists settle for the tarpan as the ancestor of all horses west of the Urals (including those of the Middle East and North Africa) and Przewalski's horse (which is not quite extinct) as the ancestor of the horses of Central Asia.

The tribes whom Julius Caesar subdued seldom fought on horse-back, though the Britons still used war-chariots which the civilized world had discarded centuries earlier. It seems likely that the horses of northern Europe were small ponies similar to our native breeds, and that the Romans brought with them larger, better bred animals. For it was from the countries around the Mediterranean – Thrace, Syria, North Africa and Spain – that the largest, fastest and best bred horses came. It is customary to attribute this to the potent Arabian strain; but Strabo, an accurate geographer writing during the life time of Our Lord, states definitely that there were then no horses in Arabia, and no archaeological or other finds have weakened his evidence. But innumerable Assyrian, Egyptian, Greek and Spanish artists have shown that the horse of those regions was, as a result of two thousand years of domestication, selective breeding and grain-feeding, a light, well-bred looking animal of 14.2 to 15 hands; and it was this horse which the Romans brought to Gaul and Britain.

These speculations are partially confirmed by excavations at Newstead, in the Scottish lowlands, which in the third and fourth century AD was a frontier post garrisoned by a regiment of Gallic horse. Most of the equine remains are of light ponies about 12.2 hands; evidently the troopers were mounted on these and, though too small for combat, they would be useful in reconnaisance and the pursuit of Pict raiders. There were also the bones of some heavier, coarser animals of about the same height – probably pack-ponies. Finally the post had a few well-bred horses between 14 and 15 hands, almost certainly officers' chargers of some Mediterranean stock.

The inventions of the saddle-tree and the stirrup reached Europe from the East during the fourth and sixth centuries respectively, and revolutionized the art of war. Cavalry could now, for the first time, charge

7

home and fight in a melee without fear of falling off. The heavy, armoured lancer now dominated the European battlefield, establishing a measureless superiority over infantry. Only in England and Scandinavia did those who could afford horses stick to the old-fashioned habit of riding to battle, then dismounting to fight on foot. The inference is that they were not good horsemen (Harold almost had a mutiny when he tried to make his Saxons fight on horseback against the Welsh) and that they had few good horses. Both suppositions are partially confirmed by chroniclers: the Venerable Bede says that it was rare for Saxons to ride before the mid seventh century, and no King of England employed a Master of Horse before Alfred (871–901). His successor, Athelstan (925–940) forbad the export of horses, which suggests that he took more interest in them; but at Hastings (1066) the Saxon Army fought wholly on foot. Such ponies as they had, for carrying them on the marsh, are shown in the Bayeux tapestry as much smaller, meaner animals than the destriers of the Norman knights.

About the knights' charger there has been much nonsense written, based on the assumption that the 'Great Horse' required to carry an armoured knight in battle had to be a great, lumbering cart-horse. The expression 'Great Horse' or destrier simply means a knight's charger, and his size must have varied from

Above, this Greek vase shows the beautiful, well bred horses of about 14.2 and 15 hands that were typical of the countries round the Mediterranean for many centuries before the birth of Christ.

Right, the distinguished head of an English Thoroughbred.

10

Left, an irresistible foal just waiting to be cuddled.

Right, an engraving of the battle of Marston Moor which shows Cromwell leading a charge mounted on a fairly small, light horse. It was he and Prince Rupert who first recognized in England that speed and manoeuvreability were essential for the cavalry if they were to be effective against musketry.

Below, the renowned semi-wild ponies of the Camargue, which are thought to possess Oriental blood and to be a very ancient breed indeed, probably descended from prehistoric horses. They are sometimes used as cow ponies to herd the black Camargue bulls.

century to century according to the weight he had to carry. From the eleventh to the fourteenth century the knight was clad in mail over a padded leather or woollen gambeson, and his horse was unarmoured. He was, by modern standards, a smallish man, turning the scales perhaps at ten stone. His mail hauberk would hardly have weighed more than twenty-five to thirty pounds. Surviving saddles of the fifteenth century weigh about forty pounds, but the twelfth century saddle probably weighed less because it carried less. Add a few pounds for helm, gambeson, lance, sword and shield, and one comes to the conclusion that the knight's charger of the early middle ages need not carry more than sixteen stone. British cavalry horses of 1914 carried between seventeen and a half and eighteen stone, assuming that the rider weighed eleven stone; French and German horses carried much more. One therefore concludes that there was no need for the knight to ride an enormous weight-carrier; what he needed was

something very like the ordinary twentieth-century cavalry horse, of about 15.2, well bred and able to gallop.

This is precisely what the Bayeux tapestry and other contemporary illustrations show; the Norman knights' destriers were well bred, hunter-type horses, if one makes allowance for the convention that an artist must show men proportionately much bigger than horses or inanimate objects – ships are depicted about the size of rowing boats, and horses as donkeys. Curiously enough, all were stallions. It was not until the late eighteenth century that the cavalryman of Western Europe realized that geldings and mares, because they are more tractable and more silent, make better cavalry horses.

At the time of the battle of Hastings, Normans had conquered southern Italy and Sicily, and some of William's mercenaries came from those distant lands, bringing no doubt their horses with them. William himself is reputed to have ridden a Spanish horse. The Medi-

terranean countries were still the source of the best horses, and the Arabian strains must by now have been strong there. For in the centuries after Strabo the Bedouin had discovered that for war the horse was a far better animal than the camel. A hard nomadic existence with sparse limestone grazing, little water and occasional feeds of barley from an oasis allowed only the fittest to survive, but mares and foals were treated by the dwellers in goathair tents almost like their own children, and fed with camels' milk even when their riders went short. Centuries of this life produced the steed which carried Islam from the Hedjaz to the Pyrenees, an animal renowned for beauty, gentleness and fire, for iron hard hooves, solid ivory bones, steely sinews, lovely arched neck, delicate head with small ears and wide nostrils, high tail carriage and unlimited courage and endurance – the Arabian horse. One of his characteristics is his pre-potency by which he transmits his best qualities to coarser breeds, and there can be little doubt that by the eleventh century the best horses in Europe had a strain of Arabian blood. Obviously this would be stronger in the south, but a picture of a Swedish king hunting in the eleventh century shows him riding a horse with obvious Arab blood.

Nevertheless the purebred Arab was probably a bit light for an armoured knight, and Crusaders, who had plenty of opportunity to acquire Arabian horses, generally preferred something larger though with a strong Arab strain. Richard Lionheart's two favourite chargers were a Cypriot and a Turcoman; and the Franks who settled in the Kingdom of Jerusalem for nearly two hundred years preferred to import Spanish horses. None of these animals bore any resemblance to the large and heavy Great Horses

described by so many historians.

Of course there were other types of horse besides the knight's charger. The rules of the Knights Templar laid down that each knight should be provided with three chargers and a hack (or palfrey): there are mentioned also pack horses, presumably heavier and slower, and jades for menial tasks such as drawing water. It is recorded that running horses (*equites cursores*) were imported into England in the twelfth century. Were these ambling hacks or race-horses? Probably the latter, used for the king's messengers and as hunters for wealthy nobles. Richard Lionheart had two such, Favell and Lyard, described as being swifter than dromedaries and destriers, which he said he would not sell for a thousand pounds. There

Below, an engraving showing the Duke of Newcastle putting one of his Great Horses through his paces in the first half of the eighteenth century. At this time these horses were only ridden by wealthy noblemen to impress their followers on ceremonial occasions.

Opposite, Polo being played during an interval at the Tehran races. It is a very ancient eastern game and originated three thousand years ago in Persia and Tibet. It only came to England in the nineteenth century, and is also very popular in the United States.

is, however, no record of him actually being offered and refusing such an enormous sum.

We have an agreeable word-picture of horsey activities at Smithfield in 1154. 'Every Friday there is a brave sight of gallant horses to be sold. Many come out of the city to buy or look on – to wit, earls, barons, knights and citizens. There are to be found here maneged destriers of elegant shape, full of fire and giving every proof of a generous and noble temper; likewise cart-horses, fit for the dray or the plough or the chariot,' (note that horses are replacing oxen for draught work). 'A shout is raised and the common horses are ordered out of the way. Three jockeys, or perhaps two as the match is made, prepare themselves for the contest; such as, being used to ride, know how to manage their horses with judgement; the point is to prevent a rival getting before them. The horses, on their part, are not without emulation; they tremble and are impatient and continually in motion. At last, the signal given, they strike, devour the course, hurry along with unremitting speed. The jockeys, inspired with thoughts of applause and hopes of victory, clap spurs to their willing horses, brandish their whips and cheer them on with their cries.'

We know that King John imported a hundred large stallions from the Continent. Coming from north Germany and the Low Countries, they were probably bought to improve the size rather than the quality of English horses. A hundred years later we find owners claiming compensation for horses killed at the battle of Falkirk, among them the most valuable was a 'bay charger with a white hind foot, value a hundred marks', the property of Sir Eustace de la Heccke; the least valuable, a black hackney of the younger brother of Sir John Botetorte, value eight marks. (A mark was nearly 35 pence but, of course, worth many times the present value of that sum.) Chargers or destriers are all valued at sixty marks or more, hacks at ten marks or less. There is on the list an animal non-committally described just as a black 'horse', valued at twenty-four marks.

In the early fourteenth century the art of war was transformed by the dramatic appearance in the

battlefields of Scotland and France of the deadliest weapon yet devised by man, the long-bow. This was not a super-accurate marksman's weapon, but a cheap instrument of mass destruction. With it a few companies of bowmen could create a beaten zone through which, under the arrow-hail, nothing could pass. Hundreds· of clothyard shafts, plunging down from the sky, pierced mail like paper, and transfixed horses, killing or driving them mad with pain and fear. The long supremacy of the armoured knight was over.

The chivalry of France tried to counter this in two ways. First, like the Vikings of old, they dismounted before battle, left their horses in the rear ready for a pursuit (in either direction) and fought on foot. This did not work because, by the time they had plodded forward four or five hundred yards in their heavy mail, shields up, shoulders hunched against the arrows which beat down upon them, they were in no fit state for a hand-to-hand fight against the enemy, fresh and in a position of vantage, who were waiting for them: they certainly could not withstand a cavalry counter-attack.

Next they tried, by piling plate armour on themselves and their unfortunate horses, to purchase immunity from the hail of arrows. But the heavy bodkin-pointed arrow took some stopping: if enough arrows rained down one would surely find a chink, a joint, or a weak spot in the armour. So plate armour became more and more elaborate, expensive and heavy, until by the late fifteenth century the knight's armour weighed as much as 100 lbs and the horse's 80 lbs. Add the weight of the saddle, now a massive affair with a pommel built up into a shield, the weapons, and the rider himself who was probably heavier than his ancestors, and you find that by 1500 the charger had to carry anything up to thirty-two stone. A horse bred to carry such a weight was an elephantine creature who could barely break into a ponderous, earth-shaking trot. Successive English kings, culminating in Henry VIII who had a personal interest in weight-carriers, took strong measures to make horses larger and heavier, importing Great Horses from Flanders and ordering the slaughter, spaying or castration of breeding stock under 15 hands. The knight had succeeded in making himself as invulnerable as a tortoise – and nearly as innocuous.

By this time gunpowder was known and even plate-armour was not proof against musket balls so the Great Horse was almost banished from the battlefield, and relegated to the tiltyard. The tournament itself, once a bloody miniature battle, became a gorgeous spectator-sport, hardly more dangerous than football. The contestants, heavily armoured, their horses protected also by great pads of straw, approached one another at a dignified trot, a barrier between them to prevent a collision, and the saddle was made without a cantle so that the rider, struck fair and square by a blunt lance, could roll off his horse without being hurt.

Nevertheless there developed in the sixteenth and seventeenth centuries, under the aegis of those great *maestri* Frederico Grisone of Naples, Antoine de Pluvinel of France and the Duke of Newcastle a highly scientific school of manege riding which was supposed to make a Great Horse handy. All the resources of contemporary equitation were devoted to getting his centre of gravity off his forehand, on to his hocks, so that he could be easily stopped and turned – horrific curb-bits armed with spikes and sharp-edged rollers, long sharp spurs, steel prickers to jab into his loins, and a couple of stout footmen with 'terrible voices' (very important, this'), and cudgels. Nothing was more efficacious, in persuading a Great Horse to move forward, than a 'shrewd cat', tied to the end of a pole and thrust, claws and teeth uppermost, between a horse's hind legs. For a nappy horse of Henry VIII Master Vincento Respini, a Neapolitan expert, prescribed a live hedgehog tied 'straitly under the tail'. It worked: the vice was corrected; but 'in such sort that they had much ado to correct the contrary vice of running away'.

The object of all this was to make the Great Horse easy to stop and

Hope you admire my teeth . . .'

Left, a young pony foal rests while its mother grazes quietly beside it, and below, Moorland pony foals playing.

turn in a melee, and then to teach him various 'airs above the ground' which were supposed to be of use in combat. The curvet, for instance, in which a horse marks time behind while raising his forehand in a half-rear, was said to be 'very necessary to make him keep his head towards an enemy'. Turning on his haunches, the volte, was 'most in use in service, especially in that manner of fight which our English soldiers term fighting at the croup'. By a half-pirouette a horse could clear a space for himself among a crowd of foot soldiers, while he un-manned a crafty enemy creeping up to hamstring him, by the *capriole*, a goat-like leap into the air accompanied by a kick with both hind legs. But all this was nonsense: cavalry actions are won not by 'airs above the ground' but by mobility, seizing the fleeting opportunity and the timing and impetus of a charge; and manege training of this kind destroyed all forward impulse. Who, inquired Thomas Blundeville, an English rider with a critical mind, wants a horse which, spurred forward in battle, 'falls a-hopping and a-dancing up and down in one place?'

Cavalry was rescued from this costly futility by Gustavus Adolphus, Prince Rupert and Cromwell who saw that the horseman's protection against musketry was not armour but speed, the ability to charge home before a second volley can be fired. For these tactics another type of horse was required. Gervase Markham, writing early in the seventeenth century was perceptive enough, while paying lip service to the Great Horse, to suggest that 'in some kinds of service in the war (especially desperate exploits to be done suddenly, or upon occurrents or discoveries, or any other kind of service wherein either the toughness or the swiftness of the horse is to be tried)' a lighter, faster horse was required, such as was used for hunting. In the English Civil War the cavalry on both sides were mounted, not on Great Horses, but on medium weight horses (mainly mares and geldings) of 15 to 15.2 hands, and the dragoons on 'good, squat dragoon cobs'.

Useless and far too expensive for

Left, a team of Shires ploughing near
Ayr in Scotland.

Below, two more Shire horses at work
on their daily delivery round. The
heavily feathered fetlocks are
typical of this breed.

war, the Great Horse was also useless as a hunter. For hunting and
for the 'wild-goose chase', (a sort
of cross-country race over obstacles,
enlivened by heavy betting), one
needed a horse that was 'long
winded, tough, hard' and, above all,
able to gallop on 'till he be in that
extremity that some suppose he
cannot live an hour, yet within two
or three hours afterwards be so
fresh and courageous as if he had
never been laboured'. By the end of
the seventeenth century enclosures
had made it necessary, or at least
desirable, for a hunter to be able to
jump – a feat unknown to mediaeval
horsemen. James II, who kept one
of the first packs of foxhounds, is
described one day as keeping 'pretty
close to hounds, though the hedges
were high and the ditches deep and
wide'. Some of his less prudent
political initiatives offended even
loyal Tories who 'wear red coats
and had jumped hedge and ditch
in all else'.

Nor was the Great Horse much
joy on a journey, for he had a rough,
uncomfortable trot. For travel,
people greatly preferred a hack with
comfortable paces, especially Irish
'hobbies' trained to amble. Some
nobles, the Duke of North-
umberland for instance, rode hobbies on journeys, but mounted a
manege-schooled Great Horse for
ceremonial rides through towns.

Unsuitable for the battlefield, for

hunting and for travel, of what use
was the Great Horse apart from
providing a rich man with a costly
status symbol and a nobleman with
a pastime for his ample leisure
hours? The Duke of Newcastle had
a straight answer to this impertinent
question. 'Some wag will ask, what
is a horse good for that will do
nothing but dance and play tricks?
If these gentlemen will retrench
everything that serves them either
for curiosity or pleasure, and admit
nothing but what is useful, they
must make a hollow tree their house,
and clothe themselves with fig-
leaves, feed upon acorns and drink
nothing but water. . . . I presume
those great wits (*the sneering gentlemen*) will give Kings, Princes and
Persons of Quality leave to love
pleasure horses, as being an exercise
that is very noble, and makes them
appear most graceful when they
show themselves to their subjects,
or at the head of an army to animate
it.'

So the Great Horse as a saddle
horse passed into history. His progeny were employed in the eighteenth century as heavy draught
horses, very necessary until roads
improved, and are seen today as the
Shire, the Suffolk Punch and the
Clydesdale. All that was useful in
his manege work was perpetuated
in High School training and is seen
to perfection today in the Spanish
Riding School in Vienna.

The period which saw the relegation of the Great Horse to draught work saw also the establishment of the English thoroughbred. This, as is well known, was produced by crossing Arab stallions (sometimes known as Turks, because they were generally imported from the Ottoman Empire) with the best English hunter mares. Neither breed was itself particularly fast, though both had fine qualities: but their progeny was unbeatable as a race horse.

Arabs, Barbs and 'Turks' had been imported into England, and even more into France, in small numbers all through the middle ages; but it needed Cromwell's methodical mind to systematize the improvement of light horses. His buyers scoured the Near East for likely stallions and brood-mares, and all ships' captains in the Mediterranean knew the quickest way to the Lord Protector's favour. Racing had, in the eyes of his more fanatical adherents, a flavour of recusancy, and was banned by the government of the Saints, but when 'the King enjoyed his own again' Charles II, who had a passion for racing, very promptly ordered that 'the seven horses of Oliver Cromwell, said to be the best in England . . . be carried to the Mews for the service of His Majesty'. He imported Arabian mares, known as 'Royal Mares' but generally not named, as well as stallions, in large numbers: the Levant Company was commissioned

to obtain annually ten of the highest quality. His expenditure on horse-flesh was denounced almost as passionately as expenditure on his amours and his Navy. It is to Cromwell's thoroughness and Charles II's extravagance that we owe the thoroughbred horse.

All thoroughbreds are descended in the direct male line from one of four Arab stallions and a number of Arab mares. Each of the stallions was of a breed recognized by Arabs as noble, but they were probably not all clean-bred. The Darley Arabian was bought in Aleppo by Thomas Darley in 1706 and brought to England three years later in the modest hope that he 'would not be too much disliked'. A bay with a 'blaze something of the largest', he is believed to be clean bred of the pure Keheilan strain. The Byerley 'Turk' was imported in 1689 and used as an officer's charger in the Irish and French wars. The Godolphin Arabian was bought in 1730 in Paris, where he was found drawing a water-cart. His name was Sham, implying that he came originally from the Damascus area, and he is believed to be of the Jilfan strain, high respected but not quite as aristocratic as the Keheilan. Fourth of the foundation stallions was the Helmsley Turk. Every race horse in the world, and a vast number of top class show-jumpers, hunters and event horses are descended from these famous stallions.

Above, two beautiful Arab stallions showing the arched neck and 'dish' nose which are perhaps the most famous of the many distinctive characteristics of this ancient breed. Both horses have been British National Champions and Mikeno, on the right, is the father of El Meluk, left.

Right, a white Arab pony frisking beside his trainer in the early morning sunshine.

The horse in the New World

CHARLES CHENEVIX TRENCH

There was once an equid native to America, but he became extinct many millennia ago. In historic times the first horses in the New World were those landed by Columbus in Hispaniola on his second voyage in 1493. They were five brood mares and twenty stallions, not of the best quality, for the knights who accompanied him were understandably reluctant to risk their chargers on such a dubious enterprise and exchanged them before embarcation for 'sorry hacks'. These were, however, quite impressive enough to overawe and conquer Indians who had never seen a horse. Later imports were of better quality, and had, of course, a strong Arab and Barb strain derived from the Moorish conquest of Spain and the trade of two thousand years. It is a common phenomenon for some animals, introduced into a country where they were previously unknown but where the conditions suit them, to increase and multiply beyond all bounds. They did so on Hispaniola, and soon it was considered quite unnecessary to import any more.

The first horses to land on the North American mainland in 1519, were eleven stallions – mounts for the cavalry with which Cortez conquered Mexico – five mares and a foal. These do not seem to have escaped and run wild, but no doubt there were plenty of escapes from the horse ranches which Cortez established after the conquest. The ancestry of the feral mustang herds of North America is also traced in romantic legend to the expedition of Hernando de Soto, a tough adventurer who in 1539 led an expedition westward from Florida in search, inevitably, of gold. Three years later, after suffering great hardships, his expedition reached the Mississippi, still vainly torturing any Indians they could catch in order to get news of the precious metal. Of the hundred and ninety horses with which he had set out, only forty were left, in a pretty poor state, when de Soto himself died on the banks of the great river. The survivors of the expedition built boats to ship the horses downstream; but progress was so slow that they landed to butcher them and dry their meat. Hostile Indians arrived before the job was finished, the Spaniards hurriedly embarked and the four or five horses which were still left alive 'began to neigh and run up and down in such sort that the Indians for fear of them leaped into the water'.

From these, perhaps, were descended the mustang herds who, by the eighteenth century, roamed the western plains in hundreds of thousands. But it seems much more likely that mustangs were descended more prosaically, from breeding stock escaped, bought or stolen from Mexican ranches.

Running wild, with neither

A highly trained Rodeo horse has the intelligent face and attractive palomino colouring which is typical of many of the Cowboys' mounts.

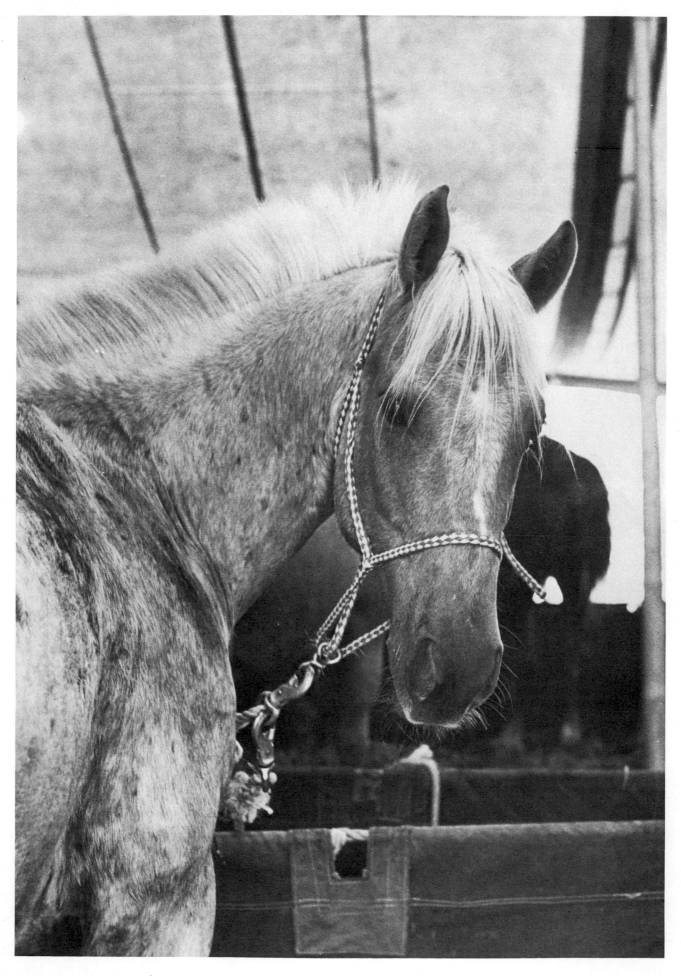

selective breeding nor grain feeding, these horses lost their good looks and degenerated in size until few were over 13.2 hands. But they retained many qualities of their Arab and Spanish progenitors – toughness, self-reliance and a singular freedom from diseases of the feet and lameness of all kinds. The Indian tribes first hunted them for meat, then learned from Spanish settlers in Mexico to domesticate and ride them. They were quick to see the advantages given by the horse in war and hunting. First to take to horsemanship were the Apaches of the south, who in 1680 massacred hundreds of Spaniards and made away with their horses: they even made armour of bull-hide, in imitation of breastplate, cuirass and morion. Then horsemanship spread all across the plains, through Utes, Pawnees and Comanches to the Blackfoot tribe along the Canadian border. In an astonishingly short time a whole new culture had developed, based on this new and invaluable acquisition. Braves buffalo-hunted and raided on horseback: they shampooed their long hair with horse-blood, made horse fat into tallow, and horse-sinews into bowstrings; they used the skin of the shins for leggings and the skin of the hocks for shoes. Horses were employed to draw the travois, for bride-prices, for ransoms and fines, for currency, for funeral celebrations and for sacrifice. Indian braves, particularly the Comanches, developed methods of catching and taming wild horses and a natural style of equitation as effective and graceful as any in the world.

The mustang herds and the Indian horse-culture for a long time made no contact with other types of horses

Two prints of Old-time America dating from the second half of the nineteenth century – right, a northern plains Indian astride his scraggy-looking Mustang pony, and below, Indians mounted on better bred and well fed animals ambush the United States Mail as it crosses the prairie.

FREDERIC REMINGTON

and another horse culture which were spreading westward from the Atlantic seaboard. French settlers in Canada, and English and Dutch settlers in New England and Virginia had brought with them the larger horses of northern Europe. We do not know much about them: presumably they brought the horses they used at home, the farmers their heavy cart-horses, the gentry their hunters and hacks. The first thoroughbred was landed in Virginia in 1730, Bulle Rock, reputedly sired by the Darley Arabian.

There was in the new colonies an unlimited demand for horses, unmatched by care in looking after them. A Jamestown parson in 1688 even reported to the Royal Society his parishioners' poor and callous horsemastership. 'They neither shoe nor stable them; some few gentlemen may be something more

curious, but it is very rare. Yet they ride pretty smartly, a Planter's Pace is a proverb, which is a good, smart, hard gallop.' To this unsatisfactory picture a French visitor added, 'All the care they take of them at the end of a journey is to unsaddle, feed a little Indian corn and so, all covered with sweat, drive them out into the woods where they eat what they can find even though it is freezing.' Evidently horses by the late eighteenth century were plentiful and cheap.

Different conditions in the New World developed some excellent new breeds of horse. Highly valued for long journeys was the Narragansett Pacer, perhaps bred from the Irish Hobby but now alas extinct. 'These are very spirited and carry both head and tail high. But what is most remarkable is that they amble with more speed than most horses

trot, so that it is difficult to put some of them upon a gallop.' Smooth paced and surefooted, they greatly appealed to intrepid 'females who were obliged to travel over the roots and holes in the New Countries'.

Virginian squires brought with them the aristocratic values of Royalist England, including a love of racing. But a full scale racecourse was expensive and difficult for widely scattered planters to construct, and the dirt roads had too many twists and turns for racing. So their races became quarter-mile sprints, on private estates or down the main street of a town. (At Lexington this became such a nuisance that it had to be prohibited by law). The sport was established before the Revolutionary War, when a traveller wrote, 'They are much attached to quarter racing, which is always a match between

27

two horses to run a quarter of a mile, straight out. . . . They have a breed which performs it without astounding velocity.'

'Without astounding velocity' . . . So the horses ridden in these races were at first not particularly well-bred. A quick start from a standstill, rather than sustained speed, was what they needed, so a Quarter-horse has well muscled quarters, rather heavy shoulders and a short back. He is a stockier animal altogether than the thoroughbred, resembling more a heavyweight polo pony, or a Portuguese bull fighting horse. Indeed the horses first used for Quarter-racing probably had a dash of Iberian blood from the Spanish settlements in the south. But speed was to be added to the mix, for all modern Quarter-horses are supposed to be descended from Janus, a stocky, thoroughbred stallion imported into Virginia in 1752. As the breed was only formally established by the formation of the American Quarter Horse Association in 1750, some of the pedigrees may well be taken with a grain of salt. But the Quarter-horse blood

needed to be constantly refined by crossing with thoroughbreds, to correct common faults such as heavy shoulders and withers, thick, upright pasterns and, in general, a tendency to coarseness.

There was in 1795 a Vermont schoolteacher called Justin Morgan, who was also a farmer, a musician and a horseman . . . or at least a man with a good eye for a horse. In settlement of a bad debt he accepted a smallish bay colt named Figure, probably thoroughbred, who made himself generally useful round the farm, won an occasional country race, made a bit of money for Justin by hauling huge logs for a wager and with all this proved to be a fast, comfortable hack. That there was nothing particular about Figure in his lifetime, that he was rather a Jack-of-all-trades and master of none, is indicated by the fact that after Justin's death, his new owner turned him out in the winter snow, like any other old horse, where he was eaten by wolves. What nobody realized until after his death was that poor Figure had excelled as a sire. Numerous first class horses were

Left, an American Paint, or Pinto Horse.

Two specialized saddlehorses from
America. Above, a Tennessee
Walking Horse in the peak of
condition – these horses are famous
for their high stepping running walk,
which is particularly comfortable for
the rider and very stylish to watch.
The prick ears, big, powerful neck,
and high tail carriage are all
typical of the breed.

Right, a Saddlebred – the 'All-
American' horse with the five gaits –
doing the Slow gait, which is
something between a walk and a trot.
The particular gait of the Saddlebred
is 'the rack', which is a flashy, fast,
four beat gait very comfortable for
the rider, but tiring for the horse.

Next page, an early print of an
Indian Buffalo Hunt. Their ponies
were Mustangs and were not at all
well looked after, so that they
became rather thin and scraggy stock.

Three of Rodeo's five main events: – top, steer wrestling is as dangerous as it is difficult and the cowboy leaps from his horse to catch the steer when travelling as much as 40 mph.

Centre, bronc riding. The riders have to stay aloft for eight seconds and if the bronc is really mean this can often prove very difficult.

Below, calf roping is a necessary art practised frequently on the ranches. The horse stands back to take the weight of the calf once the rope has found its mark, and then the cowboy leaps down to tie up the calf.

Right, a spectacular Appaloosa, or Spotted Horse.

32

identified later as Figure's get, and inherited all his versatile strength, willingness, courage and intelligence. The Morgan horse became a byword for an equine allrounder. He is generally under 15 hands, with high head and tail carriage, a deep wide chest, shortish legs, good sloping shoulders, strong quarters and a beautiful, intelligent Arab head. He should be a dark bay. In the days of horsed cavalry he made the perfect charger, sought after by 'Yellowlegs' from General Sheridan downwards, and is now one of the most popular breeds in the United States. Thoroughbred and Quarter-horse enthusiasts both claim Figure for their own, but neither have much hard evidence to support their passionate partisanship. Figure was the perfect specimen of the horse that everyone wants – the horse which does everything and costs nothing. His progeny have proved particularly tenacious of the former quality.

The Tennessee Walking horse is another example of a breed developed in America for a specific purpose. Southern plantation owners, especially those of riper years and ample bank balances, were not all dedicated to a life of hard physical exercise under a semi-tropical sun; they wanted a super-hack which would carry them quickly and comfortably while they rode between and inspected row upon row of crops before the first mint-julep of the day. By selective breeding from Morgan, Quarter-horse and Standard bred strains and patient, meticulous horsemanship, they produced a horse with three gaits, of which the third is peculiar to the breed. They are an ordinary walk, set off in show horses by a cadenced nodding of the head; an easy, luxurious canter; and an extra-ordinary running walk, smooth and high-stepping, which carried his owner along, puffing a long-ashed cigar, at a comfortable nine miles an hour with a minimum of fatigue for horse and rider.

Last of the specialized eastern saddle-horses is the American Saddle Bred, of thoroughbred ancestry, somewhat similar to the

Above, a Tennessee Walking Horse being put through his paces at a show.

Right, Trotters racing round the track at a local show in England where this sport is growing in popularity.

Tennessee Walking horse but without the famous running walk. The ordinary Saddle Bred horse has the three natural gaits, walk trot and canter, all very accurately and elegantly performed. The 'Five-gaited horse' has, in addition, two artificial gaits, which have to be taught. The 'slow gait' is something between a walk and a trot: the horse almost trots in front and walks behind. The 'rack' is a development of the slow gait, with an even rhythm and faster speed. Both are very comfortable for the rider, but tiring for the horse.

Finally, there was the eastern harness-horse – the Standard Bred, a fast racing trotter, also of thoroughbred ancestry.

In their new homes, particularly in the blue grass country where the grazing has rich food value, horses flourished, as did racing. The first formal race meeting, apart from Quarter-races, was held in Kentucky in 1788, and gentlemen were asked to come armed lest proceedings be rudely interrupted by Indians. In Charlestown race meetings soon became fashionable social occasions, with ample opportunities for duelling and dalliance; 'youth anticipating its delight for weeks, lovers becoming more ardent, and young damsels setting their caps with greater taste and dexterity . . . the *quality* of the company in attendance . . . the splendid equipages . . . the gentlemen attending in fashionable London-made clothes, buckskin breeches and top-boots.' There is a curious mixture here of sophistication and simplicity, of security and peril, of an elegant social life against a background of the silent forests and, perhaps only a few miles away, the painted Indian war-party moving swiftly through the trees. But 'horses and law-suits', observed the French Republican consul in 1793, 'comprize the usual topic of conversations. If a traveller happens to pass by, his horse is appreciated. If he stops, he is presented with a glass of whisky and asked a thousand questions.'

Meanwhile horses had spread all over the middle and far west. First, of course, there were the feral mustang herds and Indian ponies moving up from Mexico. In the late eighteenth century the Spaniards colonized California, bringing from Mexico their fine Spanish horses which were stolen in hundreds by Indian and, indeed, American raiders such as Pegleg Smith and Philip Nolan, and so came east to enrich the stock of the interior. From Canada and the eastern states voyageurs, traders, farmers and soldiers moved west, taking with them their larger horses of northern Europe. So the mustang strain was strengthened even from the early days by other breeds. Nevertheless it is probably true to say that by the mid nineteenth century, the start of the short lived 'cattle kingdom', most Indian ponies and most cowpunchers' ponies were pure mustang; but travellers tales suggest that the best generally bore Spanish brands.

The Indian was in his way a fine horseman, but a bad and utterly callous horsemaster, who regarded ordinary horses as expendible. Believing that a raw back did not hurt a

horse when it was warmed up, he thought nothing of riding an animal whose whole back was one bloody wound. He was entirely ignorant of selective breeding. Poor stallions were allowed to run wild and perpetuate their runtish stock, while good ones were reserved for riding. Only one tribe, the Flatheads, gelded colts not required for stud; and only the Nez Percés made any attempt at selective breeding to produce their peculiar 'Apaloosa', a grey with black and brown spots and vertically striped hooves. His turned-in forefeet and wide heel with well developed frog made him safe and surefooted along narrow mountain paths and over rough, slippery ground, while his thin, rat-like tail did not get caught in thorn bushes. But in most tribes the Indian pony, like the feral mustang, had sharply deteriorated from the original Spanish stock.

Nevertheless there is a school of thought which indignantly refutes any suggestion that the mustang lacked any equine virtue except, perhaps, size. It is an emotional, not an intellectual belief, akin to the nineteenth century article of faith that any red-blooded American boy could ride and shoot, particularly if he had been taught neither. But it was not an opinion much voiced in the west in 1840. No doubt there were exceptions, but the average grass fed mustang was, from the day of his first backing, a docile slug, and

small at that. To quote only an ancestor of mine, J. H. Lefroy, who was surveying in the west in 1840, and rode Indian ponies in the Indian style with nothing but a thong tied round the lower jaw, 'Though scarcely at all broken in, these horses are good-tempered, completely free from vice and much more easily managed than our own.' It is not difficult for a six foot man to ride the devil out of a 13.2 pony, which puts Indian and early western horsemanship into proper perspective. The more realistic contemporary artists show the western horse as he was in fact, not in glorious technicolor, but a small, quiet animal with a large, common head, a ewe-neck and falling away behind. Most travellers who praised the horses of the Comanches, Apaches, Shoshonis, Nez Percés and other tribes reported many Spanish brands among them. Chiefs would pay traders good prices for Spanish or 'American' horses.

Nevertheless the mustang had some excellent qualities. He was intelligent, sure-footed, tough and abstemious; capable, although only grass fed, of long journeys at a slow pace. Above all he seemed to have an inherited 'cow-sense', and instinctive knowledge, like a sheepdog's, of what a cow or a steer will do and a delight in frustrating this. Cowpunchers and Indians both achieved their mobility by the 'remuda' system, a herd of spare horses

The 'wild' Chincoteague ponies are found on the island of that name off the coast of Virginia, and are often pinto coloured. They are thought to be stunted horses, rather than ponies, as they have the head of a horse and probably their ancestors were some of the horses brought over in the early colonial times which then escaped.

accompanying those being ridden. A working cowpuncher needed for a round-up not less than seven ponies – two morning, two afternoon and two night horses, so that each rested every other day, and one spare. The U.S. Cavalry, which really knew its job and for whom the remuda system was not practicable, never rode mustangs if it could get anything else. The Royal North-West Mounted Police, the Mormon elders and most cattle barons took rapid steps to improve the horses they found in the west by the prompt introduction of thorough-bred, Quarter-horse, Standard bred, Morgan and even Percheron stallions. Not all these experiments were successful: some crosses were too large and clumsy, some did not do well on grass, some lacked 'cow-sense'. But by the end of the nine-teenth century the western horse had been immeasurably improved.

The western Quarter-horse, in particular, makes a very fine cutting horse and rodeo-performer favoured particularly in Texas: Sam Houston was a Quarter-horse lover, and in his state Quarter-horses are sometimes called 'Copperbottoms' after his favourite stallion. Many cattlemen, particularly in California and Colorado, prefer the thoroughbred, and comparing him with lesser breeds, hold that anything they can do, he can do better. This is probably true of rodeo performers: Jack Hammer, one of the greatest cutting horses

Thoroughbreds from the famous blue grass region near Lexington, Kentucky.

California ever produced, is a thoroughbred; but it may not be true of real range working horses which cannot receive the feeding and care a thoroughbred requires.

A characteristic of American horse-culture is the great stress laid upon colour, a matter in which European horsemen are generally not much interested. Apaloosas, Palominos, Albinos, even those which are known in the United States as Pintos or Painted Ponies (in England skewbalds, piebalds or 'coloured 'orses') have societies dedicated to their glorification and refinement. The Apaloosa may, perhaps, qualify as a separate breed by virtue of certain peculiarities of conformation; but the others really do not, though they are often treated as though they do. Palominos may be beautiful, and therefore command a higher price than equally good horses of less glamorous colours, but that is their only advantage.

Tradition has it that the foundation stock of all South American horses was a party of five mares and seven stallions imported in 1535 to what is now Buenos Aires and left to

run wild when the garrison, besieged and starving, evacuated the post. By 1600, so we are told, their progeny had so increased that they could not be numbered. Tiresome historians, sceptical of legend and hungry for facts, have undermined this excellent tale: why, they ask, did the starving garrison not eat the horses? Answer comes there none. It seems, perhaps, more probable that most South American horses are descended from those brought in far larger numbers to Peru and Chile between 1532 and 1560.

The pattern of horse breeds in South America is a trifle confused because in different countries different names are given to what is, to all intents and purposes, the same breed. All South American horses are descended mainly from the original Iberian stock, though thoroughbred blood has been imported from Europe, North America and Australia.

The ordinary cow horse of the pampas was a larger animal of better quality than the mustang, about 15 hands, short backed, well ribbed up but a trifle thick and

A shepherd on the plains of Patagonia in southern Argentina. His saddle is two bundles of straw covered by a sheepskin and his stirrups are wooden. His pony shows the characteristics of the Criollo ponies of this area, such as the short ears, thick neck, short back and muscular quarters. When crossed with thoroughbreds these animals make excellent polo ponies.

common about the head and neck. They were first class working horses, well balanced and tractable, with legs and hooves like steel so that they generally worked unshod. Wonderfully handy, a bit of thoroughbred blood gives them speed, and the Argentine remains about the world's best source of polo ponies – so much so that gauchos complain that their best horses are taken from them and sold at great prices to millionaires. This horse, known in Europe loosely as an Argentine, is known in that country, in Uruguay, Brazil and all over the pampas as the Criollo. He is very similar to that known in Chile as the Chileno.

The varied terrain of Peru produces three distinct types of horse. The Chola, like the Criollo, is essentially a working ranch horse, but of the hills, not the plains. He is shorter in the leg and more heavily built, very apt for scrambling up and down the mountains. The Costena is a miniature show hack, never over 14.3 hands, with a remarkable smooth, extended walk which he can maintain for very long distances at a phenomenal speed. He is wonder-

fully comfortable to ride, and deserves to be much better known outside his own country. Finally there is in the high Andes, living out of doors up to 13,000 feet in all weathers, a small, tough mountain pony known as the Morochuca.

The wonderful thing about horses in the Americas is the variety which flourish there in their original state or developed to suit local needs. Ireland may breed thoroughbreds better than any in the world, the Waler is unequalled as a working horse, the best Iberian horses may be found in Spain – but in North and South America Iberian, thoroughbred and north European working horse strains met under conditions ideal for horsebreeding, at a time when the Manifest Destiny needed the horse to carry it forward. With these various breeds, refined and specialized, is found an extraordinarily varied collection of horse cultures and schools of horsemanship. Hunting, racing, showing, jumping, rodeo and ranching are all practised to a high degree of skill, and have in the Americas the horses they deserve.

'Merry Bellsong', a handsome Morgan Horse from Massachusetts.

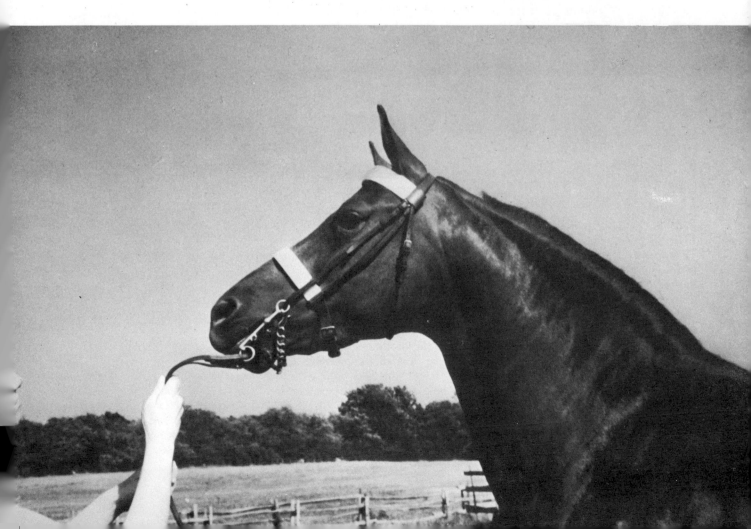

Looking after ponies and horses

ELWYN HARTLEY EDWARDS

Ponies and Paddocks, rather like the 'love and marriage', 'horse and carriage' of the popular song, go together. At any rate that is how it seems to most people, and how beautifully simple it would be if that was the sum total of keeping a pony or a horse. In practice, whilst a paddock is a necessary requirement, the ownership of one of these fascinating but infinitely helpless animals involves a lot more than the provision of an acre or two of scrubby land, producing, at best, a *kind* of herbage in summer and being reduced to an area of glutinous mud in winter. It is true that the 'natural' food of the equine is grass, but it must be available in both the right quantity and quality if it is to provide a means of sustenance all the year round.

Furthermore, the modern horse who, unlike his wild ancestors, works for his living, cannot manage entirely on grass whatever the quality. Given the same environment as the pre-domestic horse, which was unlimited acreages of grazing including grasses, herbs and shrubs in such variety as to constitute a balanced diet, and constant fresh water; and without having to work at speed and often over obstacles under the weight of a rider, the modern horse would indeed, exist satisfactorily enough. In the spring and summer when the grass was at its peak nutrient value and when the weather was warm he would grow fat and sleek; in the cold winds and wet of winter, when food was scarce, he would lose condition and strength, as did his forebears. But the twentieth century horse, afforded the liberty of a very restricted area in comparison with that enjoyed in his feral state, is expected also to gallop and jump, pursuits which call for an expenditure of energy entailing the feeding of supplementary, energy-producing foods over and above what could be obtained from a piece of grassland. In fact although ponies and paddocks go together, grass and grazing areas whilst necessary do not assume such an importance when it comes to managing the larger horse who spends much of his time in the stable.

Ponies, in Great Britain particularly, and in many other areas of the world, derive from one or other of the indigenous breeds which have inhabited the mountains and moorlands of the British Isles since time began, or, of course, they may be pure representatives of one of these nine native breeds i.e. Welsh, Dartmoor, Exmoor, New Forest, Fell, Dale, Highland, Shetland or Connemara.

Endowed with stamina and an incredible hardiness these ponies need far less molly-coddling than their larger brothers whose veins may hold a fairly high percentage of Thoroughbred and Arab blood. Indeed, the pony thrives better if kept out all the year round and is perfectly happy in weather that would reduce

A Furiso – North Star mare from the Furioso studs south of Budapest. These are striking, all-purpose horses which cross very well with Arabs and with another well-known Hungarian breed, the Nonius.

Left, a New Forest pony foal. These make very good family ponies and children's quality show or hunting ponies. The larger animals are capable of carrying light adults.

Below, one of the ancient breeds of pony that are found all over Europe. This is the native Haflinger of Austria, a sure footed mountain pony used for all kinds of pack transport.

Opposite, sweeping down the stable yard before feeding time at a school of riding in Essex.

many larger horses to shivering misery. Nevertheless, despite his toughness, a pony cannot live on air nor on a tiny, bare paddock.

To commence, what kind of a paddock is most suitable? If he is kept on his own (which is not really a good idea since most of all he needs the company of his own kind) the paddock needs to be of about three acres of well drained ground. A smaller area will do, but it means that a greater quantity of extra food will have to be given and there is the danger of a small piece of ground becoming a poached mud patch in winter. Ponies are rarely unsound but they can get mud-fever (a painful skin irritation on the legs and belly), cracked heels (when the skin becomes chapped) or thrush (an unpleasant, rotting condition of the feet caused by dirty standings) just as easily as any other equine. The grass must be of fairly good quality, of the sort found in old pasture land, and the ground and hedges free from any of those poisonous plants which are so fatally attractive to horses and ponies. The

most common poisonous plants are *ragwort*, with its yellow flower, most of the *buttercup* family, which horses will eat if the rest of the grazing is poor; *foxglove*, *monkshood*, *black briony* and, of course, the most deadly of all, the English *yew*.

Natural hedges probably make the best fences since, like trees, they afford shelter and act as a wind-break. In their absence the best fencing is wooden post and rails, but it is expensive and a fence almost as good can be made from heavy gauge plain wire stretched tightly between strong posts with the lower strand not less than one foot from the ground. Barbed wire, chicken mesh, old bedsteads and pieces of derelict motor-car are neither suitable nor safe.

If the field offers no natural shelter then one of the open types of field shelter, sited to face away from prevailing winds, is necessary; in any case it is advisable to have one in case the pony has to be kept in for reasons which will be dealt with later. It is quite probable that the pony will not use the shelter in

winter, preferring to either stand outside in its lee or under a natural protection. In summer, however, he will go into it more to keep away from the flies.

Finally, the paddock must contain no foreign bodies in the shape of cans, bits of wire, glass etc. which might cause injury, and most importantly there must be an adequate supply of clean water. A bucket placed by the gate does not constitute an adequate supply and is, anyway, too easily knocked over. Water is best supplied by a field pipe to a trough which has no sharp edges and can be emptied for cleaning, but a galvanized tank serviced by a hose-pipe will do, although it is more difficult to clean. Water, incidentally, is just as essential as solid food, after all 80 per cent of the horse's body is made up of that commodity. A horse or pony can do without food for as much as 30 days but deprived entirely of water he will die in about a quarter of that time.i

Given that such a paddock is available a prospective pony-owner

43

has a good foundation on which to commence pony-keeping. But that is all it is, a foundation.

In the summer the pony will be quite content with nothing more than grass if he is not doing very much work, on the other hand such is the perversity of ponies that too much grass is almost as bad as too little. Ponies, particularly the pure native mountain and moorland breeds, were bred originally on the sparsest of grazing and are just not equipped to cope with a large supply of lush, sweet summer grass. Being by nature ever ready to eat that which is offered they will stuff themselves until they resemble little barrage balloons on legs and the results can be disastrous. To be grossly overweight is bad for either human or animal, greater strain being placed on the organs and limbs. But an overweight pony, apart from being too fat to exert himself at anything more than a plodding walk, can contract a most painful disease of the feet which is called *laminitis* and which is an acute inflammation inside the outer protective casing of the hoof affecting the sensitive laminae. If, therefore, a pony begins to present too portly a figure one has to be cruel to be kind and deny him access to the luscious grass which he loves but which can be his undoing. Making use of the field shelter he can be confined there during the day, when the flies are in any case troublesome, and put out at night. If he still continues to put on weight then there must be a general hardening of hearts and his grazing restricted to just a few hours in each day. If he is tubby in the early part of the year he must not be galloped about until he has lost his surplus weight and is in harder condition. Galloping fat ponies is not the way to get them fit, they must be conditioned gradually and exercised at walk and slow trot, otherwise the effort can be too much for their wind and legs.

Perhaps the key to understanding the nutritional needs of the pony and horse is to appreciate that like all living creatures they utilize their food intake to fulfil what may be called the four requirements of life.

These are:
1. Maintenance of body temperature (100°–101.5°F. in the horse).
2. Replacement of natural tissue wastage.
3. Building up and maintenance of body condition.
4. The supplying of energy needed for movement and for the internal processes of digestion etc.

If food is short and the weather cold the first two requirements will take the lion's share and the last two will get next to nothing. As a result the animal gets thin and loses strength and energy. Even when food is plentiful and all four requirements are satisfied, the animal's condition will suffer if he is made to work hard and expend a lot of energy. The working pony or horse must, therefore, have an input of energy food to match his expenditure of energy if he is not to lose condition.

Energy is produced by foods like beans and peas, oats and to a slightly lesser extent barley. Maize, also, is a

heating, energy-giving food. However, these energy foods are not natural ones to the peculiar digestive system of the horse, which was designed to cope with grass and similar herbage, and they cannot be digested without bulk and roughage. In the case of the hard-worked pony grass provides this bulk quite adequately. Energy is probably best supplied by oats but unfortunately oats do not really suit ponies, since they frequently become quite unmanageable on even a handful a day, while the smell of beans and peas is enough to make them spend half their time bucking, kicking and standing on their hind-legs. The answer to the problem is to restrict the grazing to a reasonable level and feed one or another of the proprietary brands of pony nuts and cubes, which are in fact, in some instances, a complete, balanced diet in themselves. A ration of 3lbs of nuts per day mixed with 1lb of bran, which contains a high percentage of essential salts, and a double handful of chaff (a mixture of chopped oat straw and hay) and fed damped

should keep a 13 h.h. pony sufficiently energetic. Some ponies will, of course, need more and others less but this is something that can only be discovered by studying the individual concerned.

By September, in Great Britain, the grass will be losing its goodness and new growth will not occur until the following April. From this point on the pony will require hay, which should be fed throughout the winter months if he is not to lose condition. The feed that kept him sufficiently energetic in the summer will now suffice in winter when he is not doing so much work to keep him in condition. Sliced carrots, not chopped ones which might lodge in the gullet, apples etc. can be added to the concentrate feed to add variety but *not* household scraps. A pony is not a dog and his system is not designed to digest the remains of the Sunday lunch. Incidentally, if grass is short, the temptation to give the pony a treat by pressing the contents of the lawn-mower box on him is to be resisted. The pony will not refuse the offering but the result can be

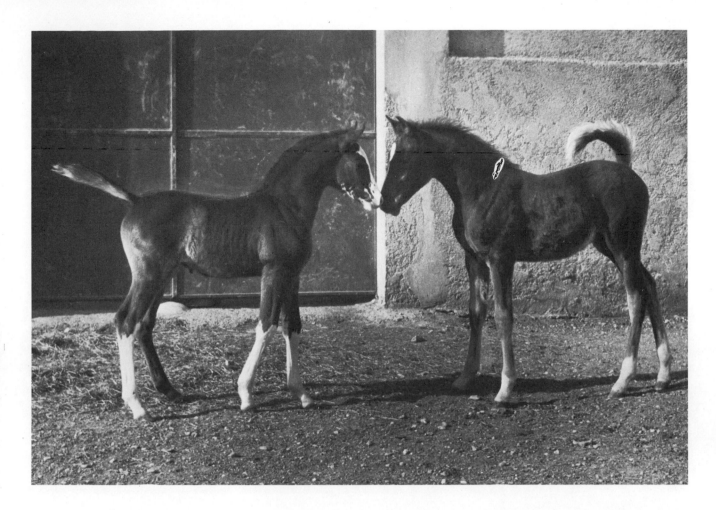

Above, two Arab foals make friends.

Left, Felabellas are the smallest breed in the world, and originated in the Argentine. This one looks minute beside his pony companion and lives in California.

disastrous and may end in a severe bout of colic (equine tummy-ache) due to the cut grass impacting in the stomach. Although ponies are sagacious little persons they will get into trouble if the opportunity to do so is presented, so it is wise to give the hay ration in a haynet (a small one in the morning and a larger one in the evening) and to string up the haynet as high as possible, well out of reach of a pawing fore-foot. Finally, a block of mineral salt, or even a good, big lump of rock salt, should always be kept in the field to provide those minerals deficient in either pasture or supplementary food.

Should a pony who is being fed and is on reasonable grazing not look well and be generally listless it will not always be because he is not getting enough food – it is far more likely that he has worms, in particular *red worms*. These parasites are always present in the domestic horse and on the pastures they occupy, the latter being the principle vehicle in their life cycle. Much can be done by managing the grass correctly, resting fields regularly and grazing them

with cattle in a rotational system. Horses are bad grazers, being very selective, but cattle are the ideal vacuum cleaner on four legs and what is more they do not act as a host to the red worm they ingest. However, management of pasture land to the degree required is quite impractical for the majority of the one or two horse owners, who can often do no more than remove droppings regularly. It is important that this should be done since it is in the droppings that the red worm eggs are passed out of the body; they then develop and ultimately regain entry into the system from the pasture and the whole cycle begins again.

Practically, the main area of attack against the red worm must, therefore, be confined to the horse itself. There are a number of proprietary medicines available in pellet form but it is probably wiser to consult a veterinary surgeon who will advise on dosage and frequency after taking an egg count from a sample of dung. Heavy infestation by red worm can result in anaemia, loss of condition to a pronounced degree and in

very severe cases death may ensue.

During September the pony will have begun to grow his winter coat which provides a virtually water-proof protection against the worst weather when it is fully grown. An important factor in the waterproof-ing is the formation of a layer of grease next to the skin, and it is therefore quite wrong to set about cleaning and grooming the pony thoroughly during the winter. All that is necessary is a quick brush over with a dandy brush to remove the worst of the mud without inter-fering with the layer of natural grease.

Possibly the most important factor in managing a pony at grass is supervision. Each and every day, whatever the weather, the pony must be inspected to see that all is well with him and that water is available. In summer leaves, twigs and scum will collect on the drinking trough and must be removed, whilst in winter there may be ice to clear from the surface.

The last item in the pony's welfare is the care of his feet which, like

our nails, grow quite rapidly. It is possible to ride ponies without shoes if they never come off soft going but in general a working pony needs to be shod if he is not to become foot-sore on hard roads and stoney tracks. Once a month his shoes will need to be removed, whether they are worn out or not, the feet trimmed and cut back, and the shoes replaced either with the old set or with a new one. Neglected feet are more prone to becoming diseased and may, indeed, cause quite severe injury if they are allowed to become too long or if the nail clenches rise up and protrude beyond the wall of the hoof. In both the last instances the pony can cut itself with its own feet.

Ponies of the mountain and moor-land breeds or those containing a large proportion of native blood will live out all the year very well but those of more aristocratic lineage, the Thoroughbred and the various Arab crosses, are not always so well-suited to the rigours of cold and wet weather and do not grow such a thick protective coat. Usually they will need stabling, at least at night, a

Above, Welsh Mountain ponies are acknowledged as the world's most beautiful ponies and owe their stylish heads to an original infusion of Arab blood. They are much in demand for harness work in the popular driving classes in America and Canada as well as children's first ponies in Britain.

Right, Dartmoor ponies are also ideal ponies for very young children, though if must never be forgotten that although these animals are tough and healthy when living wild without care and feeding from humans, they do need regular attention when they are trained and working. This confiding little pony has collected a piece of bracken in his mane on his wanderings.

48

proceeding involving much extra work, but if they have to live out it may be necessary to provide them with a waterproof New Zealand type rug – and that, too, involves a lot more work and attention. They will also need larger rations of concentrate foods than the more self-sufficient natives.

Horses, as distinct from ponies, may be expected to be in harder work and for them stabling is frequently a necessity. In days gone by, when hunting was the *raison d'être* for keeping a horse, hunters were put out to grass in May and not brought into the stable until September. The increase in competitive riding has now changed that routine and the majority of horses work throughout the year, being given only a matter of a few weeks when they are entirely at grass. In some ways this arrangement is beneficial since the horse has little or no opportunity to lose his hard condition, whereas the horse out for the whole summer becomes so fat and flabby that an extended period of quiet exercise is necessary to get him into a suitable condition to work at fast paces.

In the case of horses laid off work for the whole summer management need go no further than the provision of a shelter and regular inspection, with particular attention being paid to the condition of the feet. Usually shoes are removed altogether but it is probably better sense to shoe with 'grass tips', an attenuated form of the shoe proper, to prevent the foot breaking. No additional feeding is necessary beyond that obtained from the grass.

The management of a working horse during the summer will vary according to what is expected of him. A horse used purely for light hacking, for instance, might be stabled during the day and put out at night and would require little or no extra feeding apart from a small concentrate feed and a little hay to keep him occupied during the period spent in his box. For the horse competing regularly, however, a more sophisticated and time-consuming routine has to be devised which will be nearer to the programme carried out in the winter months. Clearly such programmes depend very much on individual circumstances and it would be difficult to suggest exercise and feeding routines tailored specifically for the hundred and one compromises which are possible. In

general a study of the management of the stabled horse in winter will provide guide-lines for the summer months.

The object of stabling horses, or keeping them under what is called the combined method, where the horse goes out for part of the day in a New Zealand rug to do his own exercising, is so that they may be more easily and effectively conditioned for a particular purpose, such as hunting.

It is possibly appropriate at this point to examine the requirements of the stable before discussing the special needs of the stabled horse in regard to feeding, exercise and grooming.

In every case a loose box is preferable to the old-fashioned stall, which involves the horse being tied up in a comparatively narrow space, facing a blank wall, for the best part of 22 hours out of 24. Nothing could be better calculated to produce a neurotic horse prone to all kinds of stable vices. The bigger the box, within reason, the better; there is less chance of the animal becoming cast i.e. lying down across a corner

and being unable to get up, and it will be more airy. Clearly, more straw will be needed to provide a bed but this should not be a consideration. It is the horse's comfort which counts.

The ideal size of box for a big horse would be fourteen feet by twelve feet but most prefabricated boxes do not exceed twelve feet by twelve feet and are seemingly quite acceptable. More important is for the box to be airy which means that the roof level cannot be too low. Up to twelve feet eaves height is desirable but not always possible, but it should be as high as conditions allow.

Doors, divided into top and bottom sections, the former being fastened back to the outside of the building or even dispensed with altogether, must open outwards otherwise it can be impossible to get into the box if either straw becomes jammed against the inside or, even worse, if the horse should get cast and be lying across the entrance.

The height of the bottom door needs to be sufficient to discourage any thought of jumping out but low

Above, two beautiful ponies with Arab blood.

Left, Debbie Johnsey and her pony Mystery XXX coming to the end of a long and arduous round in the Junior Open at Hickstead.
Beautiful ponies like this one need to be as carefully looked after as the horses that later ride in the same ring over much bigger obstacles.

51

enough to allow the horse to stand with his head out without having to crane his neck. A height of around four and a half feet is about right with a width of at least four feet. Narrow doorways are an abomination against which horses knock their hips, causing themselves considerable damage even to the extent of bone fractures. Two bolts are necessary on the bottom door, the lower one being of the kick-over type. The latter discourages the gentleman who kicks his door for the hell of it and will also frustrate the one who has learnt how to open the top bolt.

Just where boxes should be sited is of great importance. Ideally they should face south and be sited so that the inmates can see as much as possible of what is going on around them. It helps to combat boredom, the bane of the stabled horse and the source of all kinds of mischief. The next three factors to be considered are ventilation, insulation and drainage.

The first of these, ventilation, will be amply catered for if the top door is always left open but draughts, as much an anathema to the horse as the human, must be rigidly excluded. They cause aches and pains and contribute materially to colds and chills. Extra ventilation can be obtained from a window of the type that swings inwards from the base so that air enters in an upward stream and not directly on the horse, or by louvres, set high in the rear wall, to take away the rising bad air which can accumulate. Windows, of course, as well as light switches must be protected by a grill of some sort. Fresh air never hurt a horse and it is better in cold weather to give an extra rug and more feed than to shut the top door. This way colds and coughs will be avoided.

Insulation implies the use of materials which keep the building relatively cool in summer and correspondingly warm in winter. Wooden structures for this reason are best lined inside. A material to avoid is corrugated iron sheeting as a roof. It attracts heat and doesn't keep out cold. The problem of drainage is best overcome by making a slightly sloping concrete floor and an open drain *outside* the stable door.

Equipment within the box is reduced to basic essentials, a ring set in a wall for tying up and receptacles for food and water. A corner manger, made today of plastic, is very satisfactory but a heavy, galvanized tin, moved after each feed, is just as good. It is nice if one can arrange for self-filling water bowls, or afford them, but otherwise a bucket, either plastic or rubber, does just as well.

For bedding wheat straw is used and also peat moss and sawdust for those animals who delight in eating their beds to the detriment of their wind. Whatever type is used it needs to be sufficient to encourage a horse to lie down and the soiled areas must be cleaned out each day with droppings being picked up as a matter of course whenever entry is made into the box.

In the winter a long coat would be a considerable burden to a stabled horse when working hard, causing him to sweat excessively and thus lose flesh. So he therefore has his coat removed by clipping and to make good the loss is equipped with rugs to take the place of his natural

Right and below left, Highland ponies on the Island of Rhum. These sturdy creatures are now becoming popular in many countries and are often crossed with Arabs or thoroughbreds to produce first class showing animals with good bone and temperament.

Below, mare and foal almost asleep in the midday sunshine.

protection. Then, he will need feeding a balanced diet to build up his body and supply the material required for making muscle as well as producing the energy for the work he has to do. With feeding must be combined two further essential factors, exercise and grooming. The first develops and strengthens the working muscles, hardens the sinews and tendons of the legs and keeps his wind in good order. The second not only helps in the development and toning of the muscles but it cleans the body so that it can work with full efficiency.

A stabled horse, it must be recognized, is kept under artificial conditions and because of the energy demands of his work he consumes large quantities of artificial food. His body, as a result, is required to deal with a greater quantity of waste matter. Much of it will be disposed of through excrement and the in-

creased rate of breathing by the lungs, but almost as much is dispersed through the skin. It is necessary, therefore, to keep the skin clean if it is to perform this necessary function.

Although the horse is a remarkably adaptable creature, in one respect, that of feeding him, it is we who must conform to his very peculiar digestive system – he cannot conform or adapt himself to suit our convenience. Essentially his artificial diet must be as balanced as his natural one and furthermore it has to be fed to him in a way that as nearly as possible resembles his natural method of feeding. The whole digestive system of the horse who, despite his size, has a small, and from our viewpoint unfortunately placed stomach, is designed for the consumption of food taken slowly and almost continuously over long periods. It is vital, therefore,

Above, a very fit Welsh Cob circles during the dressage test at a show. These competent strong ponies are excellent out hunting and for driving.

Right, a group of hard fit Irish hunters.

that the horse should be fed *little and often*, bearing in mind that his stomach cannot cope with concentrate feeds of more than 4lbs at one sitting.

Because of the position of the stomach a second rule of feeding emerges, which is that the horse should *never* be worked immediately after a meal. Time (about one hour) must be given for the digestive process to be completed. The reason is quite simple. The stomach is placed behind the diaphragm, a section of muscle separating it from the chest cavity. This diaphragm is in contact with the lungs in front and with the stomach and liver at the rear. Immediately after a feed the stomach becomes distended and pressure, through the diaphragm, will be exerted on the lungs. This happening will cause no trouble to the horse at rest but should he be worked fast in this condition his breathing will be impaired and

interference will be caused to the digestive process. At best the horse may develop colic of varying severity, at worst the lungs could choke with blood and a rupture of the stomach occur.

For the stabled horse a balanced diet will comprise foods of three groups – *bulk*, *energy* and what may be termed *auxiliaries*. In combination these must produce five constituents: *proteins*; *fats*, *starches* and *sugar*; *fibrous roughage*; *salts*, *vitamins*, and, of course, *water* is equally essential.

Bulk is provided principally by hay, which is high in its fibrous content-matter as well as containing relatively high percentages of protein, salts, etc. Energy foods containing starches and fats, etc., as well as other constituents are for practical purposes, oats, maize, barley, etc., of which the former is preferred. Nuts and cubes, of course, can also be classified under this heading.

Auxiliaries are such items as bran, containing a high percentage of salts, linseed (a fattening food) and the various forms of *green* food – carrots and other suitable roots. In addition in this group we can include the various feed-additives, designed to repair mineral and vitamin deficiencies; cod liver oil (a conditioner), molasses, glucose and even seaweed concentrates.

The problem, of course, is in feeding the three groups in the right proportions and in this respect horses are decidedly individual making it impossible to lay down hard and fast rules. As a guide we can take it that a horse of about 16.2 h.h. will need a daily intake of food of about 28 lbs. For a horse in regular work and perhaps hunting one day per week the proportion of bulk to the remaining two constituents of the diet would be about half and half. A horse in lighter work could be given a greater quantity of bulk

food and less energy foods whilst, conversely, a horse in fast work, such as racing, would require more energy food and less bulk, although the latter will never fall below one-third of the total intake, since a large amount of energy food cannot be accommodated without its presence.

How much energy food is given relates directly to the amount of energy expended and again varies from one horse to another. In all cases, however, energy foods must be discontinued if work is forced to cease for any reason. A hunter, however, would normally be expected to be in receipt of around 10 lbs of oats per day, or the equivalent in nuts and cubes, which would be given in a number of feeds and mixed with bran, etc. The hay ration which is eaten and digested slowly is usually given in two lots, the bulk as a late feed to keep the horse happy through the night hours.

The rule about watering used to be *water before feeding* but modern practice holds that it is better to keep a constant supply of water with the horse and this is the system most usually followed.

The stabled horse, therefore, demands as much attention as a human baby and probably more! He will need feeding five times a day, at least one hour's grooming and two hours' exercise and in addition at least a further hour will be spent in making up his bed and cleaning out the stable. A certain amount of labour can be avoided by turning out the horse during the day in a waterproof, New Zealand type rug, and this is a convenient method for those whose time is limited and will reduce the period spent at exercise as well as making cleaning out an easier job. Then, of course, he has to be clipped, usually twice between October and January, and his mane and tail must be pulled and made tidy. And he will need worming at the beginning of the season and shoeing regularly.

All in all it's a far cry from the little paddock and living on grass. Who said that the horse was the servant of man?

Right, encounter between friends at the stable door.

Below, this beautiful little Arab foal is only just bigger than his companion, A Great Dane, but he is still going to risk investigating that bit of bread.

Show jumping and eventing

Left, Three Day Eventing is becoming increasingly popular and is an extremely exacting sport for both horse and rider. HRH Princess Anne was individual winner at the Burghley Horse Trials which has a difficult cross country course and which is the last event held before the Olympic team is chosen. Here she is riding her horse Doublet over the tractor tyres on the second day.

Top right, William Barker on North Flight taking a fence in style.

Bottom right, Alan Oliver has been famous in show jumping for twenty years and is still winning.

Top right, David Broome, 1970
World Champion on Manhattan.
The Championships take place every
four years and alternate with the
Olympic Games.

Below left, Harvey Smith on Archie
at the Wills Castella Stakes at
Hickstead in 1971. He rode Mattie
Brown in the Derby which he won
for the second year running.

Below, Marion Mould on her much
loved pony Stroller.

Below right, Anne Moore on April
Love in the Wills Castella Stakes at
Hickstead. This year she and Psalm
won the trophy given to the rider who
has gained the most points on one
horse throughout the season, a
trophy which Marion Mould and
Stroller held for four years
previously.

*Left, Harvey Smith on Evan Jones
at Hickstead in 1970.
Above, Marion Mould on Stroller
also at Hickstead, where she was
World Champion in 1965 at the age
of eighteen.*

*Two brilliant members of the
American team, Bill Steinkraus
(above right) who is the team
leader on his Gold Medal winner
Snowbound, and right, Mary
Chapot riding White Lightening.
She is perhaps the most stylish
member of a very elegant team and
has been one of its regular members
for many years.*

The modern horse

JUDITH CAMPBELL

The many different breeds and types of horses recognized in the world today include giants weighing more than a ton, tiny animals less than a yard high, spotted horses, golden horses, those named after their outstanding walking gait, and streamlined racing machines capable of galloping the 35 m.p.h. requisite for the Derby Stakes.

Most of the older Continental breeds trace back in some degree to the Andalusian of the Middle Ages, since Spanish horses were considered to be of the highest quality and prized throughout Europe. They originated from the crosses between local Spanish mares and the Barb stallions brought in by Moorish invaders of the eighth century, and were powerful, high-actioned horses with a very abundant mane and tail which they still retain to some extent, though they are now lighter and speedier animals than their ancestors of the Middle Ages. The modern Andalusian is almost as well known as the Spanish Arab, and the mares were used for breeding all over Europe.

Another breed which penetrated over Europe in the sixteenth and seventeenth centuries and to which many modern horses are related is the Lipizzana. These horses originally came from Yugoslavia where they are still used extensively for farm work and are prized for their stamina and co-operation. They are also bred in Austria and Hungary and have been well known for centuries for their magnificent ceremonial and parade-ground work, and it is always the grey Lipizzana stallions that perform the controlled and intricate movements of *haute école* at the Spanish riding school in Vienna. The stallions are all born black, and turn grey and finally white as they grow older, but there are also bay and chestnut horses. The different strains vary in type, and in height from 14 to 16 hands, but all make excellent carriage horses as well as riding horses – Lipizzanas were chosen and specially imported to Iran to draw the Shahanshah's Coronation Coach in 1967, and when all decked out in ceremonial harness were a truly magnificent sight.

After the last war stocks of all the various continental breeds were sadly depleted, and to strengthen them and to build up their numbers to meet the growing demand for general purpose horses, judicious cross breeding with Lipizzanas and in particular Britain's Cleveland Bay took place in many countries. The Cleveland Bay is often claimed to be the only pure-bred general purpose horse without a trace of Heavy horse blood, and originated in Yorkshire as a pack horse known as 'Chapman's Horse' which carried trinkets and merchandise over the dales. Sturdy and short-legged, the mares were first crossed with Thoroughbred sires in the 18th

The clean cut head of a Hanoverian brood mare. These horses are now being crossed with Arabs and Thoroughbreds to produce good quality riding horses.

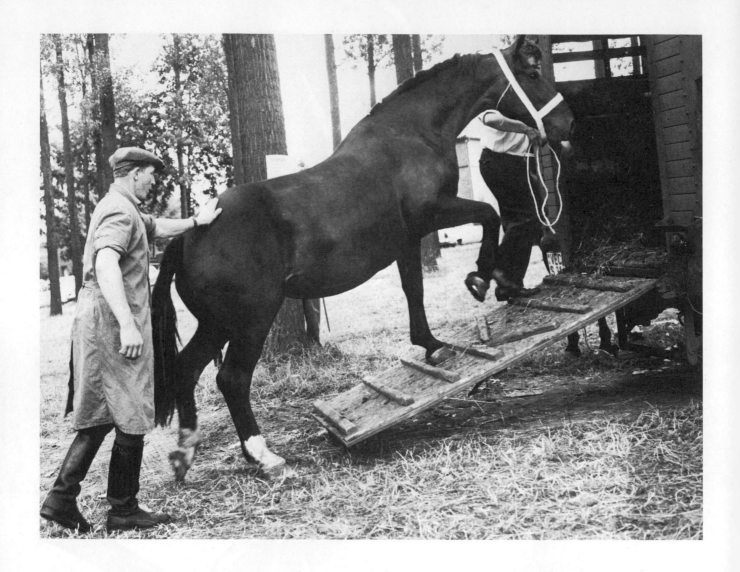

century, and by the early part of the nineteenth century the Cleveland Bay was a tall, showy carriage horse very much in demand to draw the dashing vehicles of the wealthy around London and all over the country. They make first-class heavyweight hunters, and crossed with quality mares the stallions sire excellent jumpers which are often seen in the show ring. They were first imported into America in the early part of the nineteenth century and the Cleveland Bay Society was founded in 1885. Now that both Britain and the States are undergoing a resurgence of interest in driving, it is to be hoped that the Cleveland Bay will come into his own again as a harness horse. There are many Cleveland Bays amongst the State Carriage Horses, and when the Queen visited York City in the summer of 1971 they were chosen as the local breed to draw the carriages taking part in the procession in

preference to the Windsor Greys.

One of the breeds that was strengthened with Cleveland Bays is the Oldenburg, a German horse rather heavier than the Cleveland which was not available outside Germany until 1968, when a team was purchased for the Queen. This was probably because their numbers were being carefully built up after the war, as were those of the Hanoverians, which were badly needed for work on the land in the immediate post-war years, and are now being crossed with Arab and Thoroughbred stallions to produce good quality riding horses which will compete successfully in Eventing and on the Show ground. But the most popular German horses are the Trakehners, which have been famous for their endurance and courage ever since the horses of the well-known Trakehner Stud in East Prussia undertook a nine hundred mile trek to escape from the advanc-

An Oldenburg gelding. Oldenburgs are very popular in Germany and make good working, driving and riding horses.

ing Russian armies. They are more elegant than the Hanoverians and make excellent riding and showing horses.

The Swedish Saddle Horse is one of the most recently developed of the all purpose riding horses, and contains Arabian, Thoroughbred, Trakehner and Lipizzana blood. They have been selectively bred since the beginning of the nineteenth century for temperament as well as conformation, and are as a result a very elegant, equable riding horse, up to weight and with the scope for International competing, and equally popular with civilians, the Army and the Police. Other of the better known all purpose European Breeds are the Polish Poznan and Mazuren (originally Trakehner), and the Polish Arabs which are very carefully bred and are much in demand, the Dutch Friesian and Gelderland, the Danish Frederiksborg, and the Russian Budjonny.

The settlers in the eastern colonies of America imported most of their horses from England, and under the different conditions and by selective and cross-breeding of these, combined at times with some Mustang blood, they gradually evolved the many distinctive American breeds of today.

Trotters

The American Standardbred, of Thoroughbred type but sturdier, with a longer back and shorter legs and averaging 15.2 hands, is the outstanding harness racer in the world today. It is very fast and has great endurance, and can be either a trotter, which has a diagonal action, or a pacer (which moves its legs laterally like a camel). Although these horses possess a lot of Thoroughbred blood, they also trace back to Harddravers, the Dutch trotting breed, and to a famous Norfolk Trotter imported in 1822.

In many Continental countries, Germany, Italy, Finland and Scandinavia, and particularly in Holland where the sport began, trotters and pacers are held in as much, sometimes more esteem as flatracing and steeplechasing horses. In France this form of racing started in 1836,

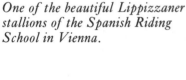

One of the beautiful Lippizzaner stallions of the Spanish Riding School in Vienna.

and of the many thousands of trotting horses now registered in that country the majority are Noram Trotters, or Demi-Sangs which are raced under saddle as well as in harness. The old sport of harness racing was once very popular in the North of England, but although it is being revived to some extent, the British racing trotter has little prestige compared with its European counterpart. Russia's well-known breed, the Orlov-Trotter, was crossed with the American Standardbred to produce the comparatively new and very fast Métis Trotter. With the North Swedish Trotter, Sweden has the distinction of possessing the only 'cold blood' horse of this category in the world.

Harness racing is a hot favourite in New Zealand and Australia, and both countries have produced trotting and pacing speed records to vie with, and in some cases surpass, those of America. Meetings are often held at night on flood-lit tracks, and it was this innovation that really popularised the sport, just as it did in Canada and America.

Hackney Horses are also harness trotters, of an old British breed with much the same origins as racing trotters, but their brilliant, extravagant action is nowadays confined almost exclusively to the Show Ring. Hackneys have been extensively exported, there are a number of foreign studs, and these handsome, fiery creatures can be seen at many European shows and at those in Australia, South Africa, Canada, the United States and South America.

The Missouri Fox-Trotting Horse of America trots behind but walks nimbly in front, producing partly through inheritance, partly through training, the low, sure-footed broken gait from which it gets its name. The running-walk of the Tennessee Walking Horse is said to be the most comfortable of all paces, and these horses and their gait were evolved especially as a mount for the cotton planters. The horses were bred up from various sources including Morgans, Thoroughbreds and the American Saddle Horse, and as foundation sire, a trotter called Black Allen that was foaled in 1886, and are now rather like a shorter, sturdier version of the American Saddler.

Other saddle breeds
The American Saddle Horse, sometimes called the Kentucky Saddler, makes an excellent riding horse for most purposes, but is now bred

A competitor at the Helsinki race track where trotting is very popular.

chiefly for the show ring where it is often an admirable exponent of the five gaits, trot, canter, rack, slow gait and walk. These horses have great beauty and tremendous presence, and as well as being the showiest of almost all breeds they also have gentle natures and considerable stamina.

A versatile American breed that is equally popular in Canada and rapidly becoming so in Australia is the Quarter Horse, an old type used for Quarter Mile racing in the eighteenth century, but was only registered in 1940. When ousted from racing by more conventional tracks and the Thoroughbred racer, the Quarter Horse pattern was preserved in a slightly modified form

in the south-west, principally in Texas where they are now extensively bred. They are low and compact with great muscular strength, particularly in the thighs and quarters, and possess an intelligent, calm temperament. They make first-class all-round saddle horses and the finer strains are still raced over short distances, usually the traditional quarter of a mile, a sport that has spread from the States to Canada, and is starting up in Australia.

For working stock the Quarter Horse has few equals and his speed, stamina and ability to make lightning turns, combined with an instinctive cattle sense, make him a specialist in the art of competitive Cutting, so popular in all three

A handsome Hackney Horse in the show ring.

countries. This sport, which grew from everyday work on the range, requires the rider to sit still and allow his horse to take over once the marked steer is cut out from the mob. From then on the Quarter Horse, crouched like a coiled spring on his haunches, watches and counteracts every move of the beast and behaves and works much like a trained sheepdog.

Within the last fifty years a vogue has started for promoting and registering horses and ponies of the same specific colouring, although often of different type. The majority of the Societies and Associations with this aim are in America and Canada, but in 1963 the British Spotted Horse and Pony Society was revived to encourage breeding of animals showing the same unmistakable, attractive coat patterns.

Appaloosas are the most well known of the American spotted breeds, and this particular colouring was developed by the Nez Percé Indians, a tribe living around the Palouse River districts of the far north-west. The horses have a parti-coloured skin, and striped hooves. The patterns of spots vary, the most usual being dark spots scattered over a white patch on hips and loins.

Red Indians always seemed to appreciate horses of spectacular or 'broken' colouring, partly for the fine show they made, partly because the light and shade of the coat pattern acted as natural camouflage, but in the States the two-coloured Pinto or Paint horse has only become generally popular in recent years. Two variations are now recognized, the black and white Overo, and the Tobiano, which is brown and white or white with any colour except black. These colourings, in Britain known as piebald and skewbald, have always been favourites with gypsies and tinkers, especially in Ireland, but it is a liking shared by many people other than the 'travellers'.

The metallic glint of a Palomino horse is perhaps the most attractive colouring of all. In the fifteenth century these golden horses are said to have been much prized by the Spanish Queen Ysabella, and they

Above, the Queen's Cleveland Bay Carriage horses. Cleveland Bays were the main breed of smart carriage horse in Britain at the beginning of this century, and were also used to build up stocks of the various continental breeds.

Right, one of the rare true-bred Exmoor ponies walking stylishly round the ring at a show. The thick neck, small ears peeping out of a flowing mane, and small, neat head with wide nostrils are distinctive characteristics of the breed.

are sometimes known as Ysabellas. They do not yet breed true and a registered Palomino may also be a registered Quarter Horse for instance, but their beauty lies in the varying shades of dun-gold set off by a white mane and tail, and each animal must also be a fine specimen of its particular type. In Britain the Palomino is promoted by both a Society and a Breeders' Association, and in America the Palomino Horse Breeders' Association, founded in 1946, will not consider registering any animal showing 'coarse, draft horse, Shetland or Paint breeding'.

There are few breeds of horse or pony that have not at some time been improved with Arabian blood. These lovely animals with their distinctive concave profiles, tapering muzzles, broad foreheads and big, luminous dark eyes, are the oldest unadulterated breed in the world. Their known history dates back to the seventh century, and they remained unsullied because they come of a relatively small stock of much prized horses, fanatically inbred, culled, and kept 'asil' (purebred) for centuries by the desert tribes. When the Arabs set out on conquest they augmented their cavalry with local horses and their stallions bred with these, helping to found the general type of 'hotblood' horse established from North Africa to Spain, and in India and the Near East. However alien horses were never taken back to adulterate their own pure Arab strains.

Very few of the cherished Arabian mares ever left their country of origin, but through the centuries many stallions were exported. Foreign breeders therefore often built up studs using domestic mares and there are not many of the true, ancient blood-lines left. Some famous studs, however, in Britain, the U.S.A. and elsewhere outside Arabia, were built on pure-bred Arabian horses, though they possibly are not considered 'asil' in Arab estimation, since different feeding and environment often produce much larger animals than the original and in some countries, particularly America, the big Arabian horse in any case is considered preferable. Although these retain many of the qualities of their breed, they differ materially from the smaller pure desert-bred horses of the Royal Jordanian Stud, which are now world famous.

Barb horses are fast, light, desert animals which come from Algeria and Morocco, but lack the Arabian's distinctive characteristics. There are few true bred Barbs today, but the ancestors of many European and New World breeds had barb blood since they were imported in large numbers in the Middle Ages, as were Arabs and Turks.

The Iranians claim their straight-profiled, tall Persian Arabs are an older breed by some 2,000 years than the desert Arabians of the Near East, though there is a theory that an ancestor of those notable desert horses known as Akhal-Teke in Russia and Turkoman in Iran, was the part foundation stock of both species of Arabian horse. The Turkoman, bred south-east of the Caspian Sea, is one of the best known Iranian breeds, although now that the Turkoman tribes have forsaken a life of nomad horse-breeders to become prosperous farmers, the great herds of fine horses that formerly roamed the steppe are no more. Turkoman horses are in much demand for racing. They are fast, built on greyhound lines like all true desert breeds, and have great stamina. In 1935 the first three horses home, in a race of 4,300 kilometres from the Iranian frontier to Moscow, were Turkomans; they took 84 days, and finished the last 500 metres at full gallop!

Although Iran is rapidly becoming more mechanized, a Royal Horse Society has recently been formed to preserve the heritage of a country which has been raising fine horses for over 3,000 years, and one type that is registered is the variation of Persian Plateau horse, the Darashuri, that is well known as an excellent saddle horse. From time to time foreign breeds are imported to the Imperial Stud at Farahabad, outside Tehran, and several of the fiery Persian Arabs stabled there have Thoroughbred blood in their veins.

The Thoroughbred is a comparatively young breed originated in

A Quarter Horse showing the powerful chest and quarters of its breed, perhaps the most versatile of any.

The favourites of the pony world are the Shetlands, and they are now making a name for themselves in America.

England by the crossing of a few imported Arabian stallions with good Hunter mares, and there are now famous studs in many countries including New Zealand, Australia, the U.S.A. and France, where the admirable cross of Thoroughbred/Arabian called Anglo-Arab, now breeds true. In conformation, grace of line and speed the Thoroughbred has no equal, the name is now synonymous with racehorse, and these horses are used extensively to develop or improve other breeds. But Thoroughbreds do tend to be nervous and highly strung, and though their quality and jumping ability fit them in many ways for sports other than racing, a Thoroughbred cross, often a half or threequarter-bred, usually proves more suitable for Eventing and Show Jumping.

In Australia many modern breeders are concentrating on Thoroughbred and light bloodstock in preference to the versatile type of animals called Walers from New South Wales. The foundation stock of these horses included hot-blooded Cape Horses brought in by traders in the late eighteenth century, and later they gained strength and stamina from cross breeding with heavier animals, often imported Clydesdales. By 1825 they were being used by the First Trooper Police in New South Wales – a force that played a big part in founding the dominion – and were

admirably suited to the rough work in the 'outback'; later thousands of them were drafted for general service with Army units, both in India and during the First World War. They make good stock and riding horses, do well on Endurance rides and are first-class jumpers – in 1940 a Waler made the then world high jump of 8 ft 4 ins. They also have the not always enviable reputation of being better at bucking than American Bronchos. But although there are still Walers at work on many sheep and cattle stations in their native land, and some units of the Australian Mounted Police still ride them, this utilitarian type is now unfashionable, which is a pity in view of their long and distinguished history.

Heavy horses

Many world breeds have a drop or two of Clydesdale, or of Shire or Suffolk blood in their veins, and these are some of the breeds of big powerful horses that were essential to agriculture and heavy draft until they were supplanted by mechanization. After World War II it seemed that heavy horses were a thing of the past, except for those still indispensible to a few Continental countries, and the animals kept for showing. Yet a short while ago interest began to revive and their numbers, chiefly in Britain and North America, are slowly increasing.

Quite a number of British and American breweries are discovering that the use of heavy draft horses to deliver beer in the major cities is not only an excellent advertisement but also more economical on short haul than using lorries. A very popular spectacle in London has been Lord Mayor's Day, and since 1954 a brewery has supplied six splendid grey Shires to draw the four and a half ton Lord Mayor's Coach through the City streets. Also some farmers find it good policy to supplement tractors with a horse team, mainly for carting feed and for use when soil and weather conditions preclude weighty machines. And although ploughing is now normally a province of the tractor, there is at least one 'horses only' ploughing

Quarterhorse mares and an Appaloosa colt being fed on the stud farm recently established in Australia.

match in England, and even a few farms left which are still entirely reliant on literal horse power. In the East Riding of Yorkshire one farmer is using a big American Gang Plough, drawn by a double tandem, to excellent effect.

American shows are well supported by the Heavy Horse breeders and the competition is keen. As in Britain the 'Heavies' are used for both publicity and work, big horses are still in demand for logging where forest conditions can immobilise mechanical labour, and they are also used for such pleasure occupations as sleigh-riding, hay-rides, trekking, and the pulling contests.

The British Shire, as befits his ancestry, is the largest, pure-bred horse in the world. A modern Shire can shift five tons with ease, and his enormous strength, stamina and docility were some of the qualities progressively stabilised and improved after the Shire Horse Society was formed in 1878. These horses are still being exported to some American states, but like the Suffolk are now less common the other side

of the Atlantic than the Belgian, Percheron and Clydesdale.

There are two half-bred Suffolk Punches in the Royal Mews at Buckingham Palace at the present time, and this is an ancient breed which has always been noted for its good trot. In Elizabethan times strong 'punchy' short-legged horses, less handsome than the modern version but of similar type, were needed to draw the first cumbersome coaches along the rutted tracks of England. Nowadays the excellent workers called Suffolk Horses or Suffolk Punches that are always coloured some shade of chestnut, are exported to the Argentine, Canada and to the U.S.A. where the several breeders have formed an American Suffolk Horse Society.

Scotland's heavy horse, the Clydesdale, originated in the Clyde valley during the eighteenth century, when native mares were crossed with Flemish stallions to give more weight. A little leggier than Shires these horses have a free action that especially suits them to draft work. Introduced into America about 1879

A typical Australian 'Waler', 16.2 hands high, used by the New South Wales Mounted Police.

Clydesdales were, and still are used for general work, and like all the heavy breeds are sometimes cross-bred with light horses to produce good heavy and middle-weight hunters and jumpers.

The Netherlands and France have always been heavy horse countries and remain so today to a larger extent than elsewhere. The Belgian Heavy Draft, the modern representative of the old Flemish horse, has been bred in a number of American states since 1866 and now provides seventy per cent of America's heavy horse population.

Percherons, another heavy breed especially prevalent in the U.S.A. and Canada, originated in the La Perche region of France, and are valued for their hardiness, activity and good temperament. These attractive grey or black horses were first imported to America in 1839, though the Percheron Horse Society of America was not established until

1905. The breed is widely distributed and there are Percherons in both Australia and Russia, but they only arrived in Britain in 1918 – after the thousands of pure and half-bred animals, brought over to France from Canada, the U.S.A. and the Argentine for Army Transport with the British Expeditionary Force, had more than proved their worth. These horses are no longer common in Britain, but a few British-bred Percherons have recently been exported to introduce fresh blood into the Canadian and American studs.

Ponies

Many hunters, jumpers and Event horses owe their hardiness and ability to extricate themselves from tricky situations to a pony somewhere or other in their ancestry, but the exact definition of a pony, as such, is elusive. As a generalization it cannot be based entirely on height

Above. Mustering cattle on the downs in Queensland, Australia.

Right, a Budjonny mare and foal from the Rostov State studs in the USSR. This is a fairly recent breed of horses and is mostly a cross between the thoroughbred and the Don Horse from the Steppes.

Above, this striking animal is an Achal-Teké stallion from the USSR and his coat is the colour of burnished gold. These are true desert horses and are a very old breed, probably closely related to the Persian Arabs.

Opposite page, top left, an American Standardbred competing in a harness race.

Top right, one of the powerful Shire Horses that are still used for ploughing in some parts of Britain.

Bottom, the golden glint of the Palomino is quite unmistakeable and can occur in any breed.

or conformation, pony type or temperament, but is a subtle combination of the lot, with different breeds having their own particular characteristics.

The history of the lovely little Welsh Mountain pony is lost in antiquity, but its looks show some Arabian ancestry. These ponies do not exceed 12 hands and have acquired an innate hardiness, courage and intelligence from running semi-wild on the Welsh hills for centuries. They are the foundation stock of the Welsh Pony (Section B, up to 13.2 hands), the less familiar Pony Cob (Section C, same size), and the handsome versatile Welsh Cob.

The Welsh Mountain goes well in harness but in Britain is generally thought of as a good though spirited mount for small children. This

outlook is applied to all British pony breeds and restricts them to only a few show classes. Elsewhere, 'performance' classes are very popular, and in South Africa, where Welsh and other British ponies are in growing demand, many shows also feature classes for part-bred and 'Handy' Welsh ponies. There are now several studs of American Welsh Ponies in the U.S.A. and most shows incorporate Pleasure Classes, driving, jumping and Western-style for this and other pony breeds.

New Forest ponies come of an ancient mixed stock, but are now bred true, and are valued as excellent 'all-rounders' of equable temperament. The modern trend is for larger ponies of more quality than the old-fashioned Forest type, and these are also bred in Denmark

and other countries. The sturdy all-purpose Fjordings of Scandinavia, good-natured ponies with shaped, upright manes, and the indispensable strong little Iceland ponies, of exceptional homing instinct, belong to the same Northern group as the Swedish Gotland, and Britain's well known Exmoor. This old, pure breed run wild on their native moorland and are easily distinguishable by their characteristic wiry winter coat, and mealy colouring on belly, muzzle and around their typically prominent 'Toad' eyes. Most of the ponies running on nearby Dartmoor are now crossbred, but a number of studs preserve the qualities of the true Dartmoor, one of the best and most attractive of the smaller riding breeds.

The sturdy, sure-footed packponies that were led across the fells and dales of Northern England during the seventeenth and eighteenth centuries have been developed into the exceptionally strong, utility Dales pony, and the smaller, lighter Fell. These ponies are good for every kind of work and like the Highland, for centuries the Scottish crofter's helpmate, have come into their own in the modern world through the vogue of trekking.

Ireland's Connemara is another of the larger breeds, an admirable riding and jumping pony, hardy and versatile, that has acquired quality from Spanish blood introduced in the Middle Ages and later, from the Arabian sources. Until recently not well known outside Ireland, Connemara ponies are now being bred in England and elsewhere.

With the exception of Falabellas, miniatures under seven hands developed in the Buenos Aires province, Shetlands are the smallest ponies in the world. Indigenous to Orkney and Shetland they are now so popular in many European countries that Dutch-bred Shetlands are actually being exported to England. For a long time they were the only pony breed known in Canada, but the Canadian Pony Society now recognizes Welsh, Dartmoor, Highland, Fell, Exmoor, New Forest and Iceland ponies as well. American Shetland ponies are shown under three types, Riding, Harness and Draft, and are matched in harness trotting races. Some have been 'modernized' and these fast, spirited and comparatively leggy creatures bear small resemblance to the docile, shaggy little ponies so often ridden by quite tiny children throughout the countryside in Britain and elsewhere in Europe.

Left, a proud Prezwalski stallion. These ponies are still found wild in Mongolia and are considered to be part ancestors of all breeds of horses.

Below, Mikeno, a Champion Arab stallion.

Few European countries possess an indigenous breed of pony, though the Haflinger of Austria and South Germany could be described as such, and is a typical mountain pony of much the same origins as Italy's larger Avelignese. They are widely used for agriculture and winter sleigh work, and several of them, with their innately calm disposition and compact strength, are proving successful in England as mounts for the heavier disabled riders.

France's 'wild white horses' of the Camargue are sometimes described as large ponies, but either way they have lived for centuries semi-wild in the marshlands at the mouth of the Rhone. They are still used for herding the black Camargue bulls, and for treks connected

Left, Dale ponies are one of the largest breed of British pony, and have a long history of hard work hauling loads in the Northern mines. They were crossed with Clydesdales to make them heavier and stronger and are true utility ponies.

Below left, a handsome black Pecheron stallion.

Below, a handsome Connemara champion pony at a show. This is one of the largest of the pony breeds and is rapidly being acknowledged as a splendid riding and, jumping pony for children and lightweight adults in many countries outside its native Ireland.

with the rapidly developing tourist trade.

Mongolian, Chinese and Tibetan ponies, and the Indian hill ponies of the Himalayas, differ slightly from country to country and region to region, but basically they are the same, small, tough, frugal living and immensely strong, and are still used for every kind of work.

The famed Basuto ponies that commanded such respect during the Boer War, have degenerated to some extent through the circumstances of modern life. They are descendants of the Cape horse, and have Persian, Arab and Thoroughbred ancestry. They first arrived in Basutoland as the result of nineteenth century Zulu raiding, and are still some of the hardiest and most sure-footed of ponies, capable of fast speeds up and

down rough mountain tracks.

The Pony of the Americas, the youngest breed of all, described as 'a happy medium' of miniature Quarter Horse-cum-Arabian with Appaloosa colouring, was first registered in 1954. The ponies were specifically evolved as handy, intelligent and equable mounts of 11.2 to 13 hands, for children up to 16 years old. They are equally at home drawing a sleigh, competing in jumping or Western-style classes or acting as the family stock horse.

When pre-historic man enlisted horses to his benefit, he ensured their remaining indispensable for nearly 4,000 years. Now, although their function changes with time and conditions, horses and ponies are still important to an enormous and growing number of people.

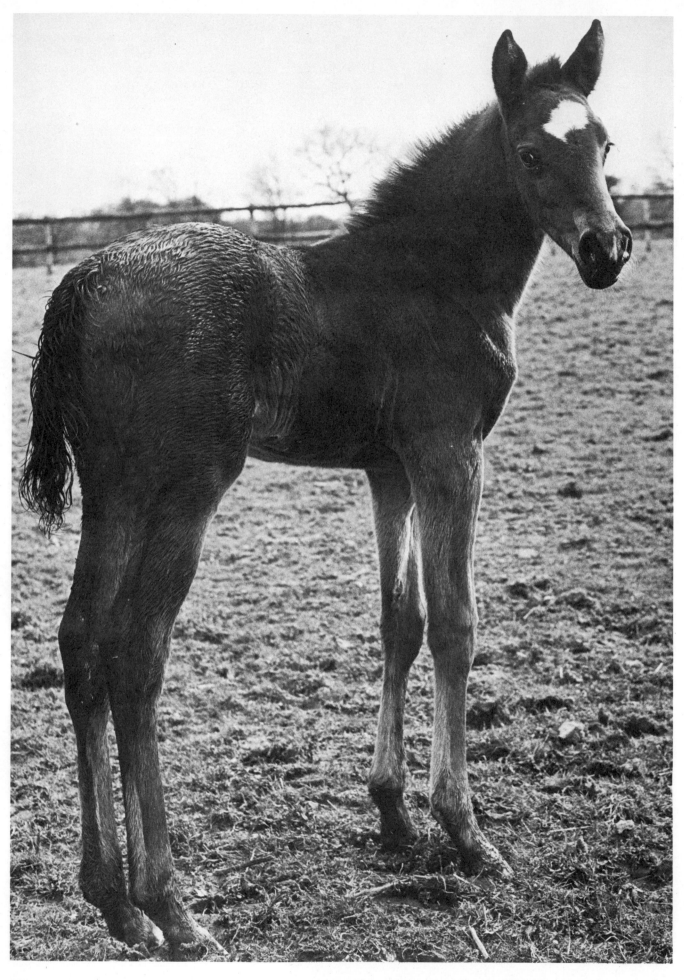

Thoroughbreds and racing in Britain and Europe

MICHAEL SETH-SMITH

At the Battle of the Boyne in July 1690 when the armies of William of Orange defeated the supporters of his father-in-law James II, the Sixth Dragoon Guards were under the command of Colonel Byerley. The Colonel's charger, which he had acquired whilst fighting against the Turks in Hungary, was the object of admiration and envy for he had the blood of countless generations of Eastern stallions in his veins, and was swifter and sleeker than the clumsy and ill bred horses which comprised the English cavalry. If the charger had been killed amongst the confusion and gunsmoke of the battle Racing would have suffered by his loss, for on his return to England he was sent to stud firstly in Co. Durham and later in Yorkshire where he founded a dynasty. Almost all modern thoroughbreds are descended in the male line either from him or from two other famous stallions – the Darley Arabian and the Godolphin Barb – both of whom had chequered careers before they arrived in England.

The Darley Arabian was bred by the Anazeh, a tribe of heroic horsemen who lived on the edge of the Syrian desert, and was reputedly a horse of exquisite symmetry, with a curved neck, a long head, three white stockings and a large white blaze. In 1704 he was sold by Sheik Mirza II to Mr Thomas Darley, the English Consul in Aleppo. As soon as the agreed price of three hundred golden sovereigns had changed hands the dishonest Sheik left the town, having given instructions that his heavily guarded prize stallion should not be removed from the Royal stables under any circumstances. Mr Darley outwitted the Sheik by arranging for a party of sailors from a British man-o'-war to row ashore at dead of night, overpower the guard, and return with the stallion to the ship. The mission was successfully accomplished, and the irate Sheik not only had his Stud Master tortured to death, but also wrote to Queen Anne bitterly complaining that 'my incomparable Arabian is worth more than a King's ransom and he was foully stolen from me by your subjects'. The Sheik was correct in appreciating the value of his stallion, whose great great grandson was the immortal Eclipse.

Twenty years after the Darley Arabian was brought to England the Godolphin Arabian was foaled. He was given as a present by the Emperor of Morocco to Louis XIV King of France and subsequently bought in Paris by Mr Edward Coke. When Coke died in 1733 he bequeathed all the brood mares at his Derbyshire home to Lord Godolphin – and his stallions to another friend from whom Godolphin bought the imported Barb, who was a bay horse standing 14.1½ high, with a pronounced crest and a rather dipped back. When he died in Cambridgeshire in 1753 cakes and

This young thoroughbred foal will be trained as a racehorse as soon as he is old enough, meanwhile he has been enjoying himself rolling in the mud.

A painting by John Wootton dated 1731 of the Godolphin Arabian with an Arab groom.

ale were distributed at his burial. Although he only served seven or eight mares a season, his influence on breeding was immense, for the bloodlines now represented by the progeny of Hurry On and Precipitation can be traced back to his grandson Matchem.

At the time that these three stallions arrived in England, horse racing was in its infancy, despite the enthusiasm of the Stuart monarchs which had made the Suffolk village of Newmarket famous throughout the kingdom, and Queen Anne's inauguration of Ascot races in 1711. During her reign twenty four Eastern stallions, nine Arabians, eight Barbs from Algeria and Morocco, and seven Turks were imported. Some of these stallions, none of whom had as great an influence upon future generations of bloodstock as the Darley Arabian, the Byerley Turk and the Godolphin Barb, were acquired on the order of Tregonwell Frampton who had been appointed Supervisor of the Royal Race horses at Newmarket by William of Orange. Not without justification is Frampton recognized as 'The Father of the English Turf', for he was virtually the arbiter of all matters appertaining to racing in the era prior to the advent of the Jockey Club, which was not founded until twenty years after his death.

The first member of the Royal family to be elected to the Jockey Club was King George II's second son, William Augustus, Duke of Cumberland. Although described as a man 'proud and unforgiving . . . who despised money, fame and politics, yet loved gaming, women and his own favourites' his contribution to Racing was remembered long after his defeat of Bonnie Prince Charlie at Culloden was buried in the annals of history, for he bred Herod and Eclipse, who was a great great grandson of both the Byerley Turk and the Darley Arabian. Herod was one of the fleetest racehorses in the land and sired a prodigious number of winners including Highflyer who was given his name as he was foaled in a paddock surrounded by highflyer walnut trees. Highflyer was never beaten, and eventually

became the property of the well-known bloodstock dealer Richard Tattersall who wisely mated the stallion with mares sired by Eclipse. So successful was Highflyer that when he died Tattersall had engraved on his memorial stone 'Here lieth the perfect and beautiful symmetry of the much lamented Highflyer, by whom and by his wonderful offspring the celebrated Tattersall acquired a noble fortune, but was not ashamed to admit it'.

In 1750 the Duke of Cumberland exchanged one of the Arabian bred horses from his Cumberland Lodge stud in Windsor Great Park for a brown yearling colt named Marske, which had been bred in Yorkshire and whose dam was a grand-

Two horses pull out in front of the rest of the field as they come into the last furlong at Lingfield.

Four horses whose names have made racing history:

Left, a portrait of Eclipse by George Stubbs painted in 1786. Eclipse was unbeaten in his racing career.

Below, winner of the Derby in 1836, the year this picture was painted, Bay Middleton stood nearly two and a half inches taller than Eclipse. Notice that jockeys rode with long stirrups until the American 'racing seat' was introduced at the end of the nineteenth century.

daughter of the Darley Arabian. When Marske retired to stud at the end of his racing career, he was not deemed worthy to serve the Arab mares, and was only used for farmers' mares at a fee of half a guinea, and half a crown the groom. Later he was allowed to serve the more valuable mares including Spiletta, a grand-daughter of the Godolphin Barb. On all Fool's Day 1764 Spiletta gave birth to a small colt foal. On the same day occurred the most total eclipse of the sun ever recorded so it was not surprising that the foal was given the name of Eclipse.

The Duke of Cumberland had been dead for nearly four years when Eclipse made his racing debut at Epsom in May 1769, but such was his reputation that he started a 'red hot' favourite and won with ridiculous ease. During the next two years he ran 26 times and was never defeated. His owner, Mr Wildman, who had made special efforts to buy Eclipse when the Duke of Cumberland died was later hoodwinked by the notorious Captain O'Kelly, who, having purchased a half share in Eclipse, proposed that he should purchase the other half for either £1,000 or £2,000. He showed Wildman three notes for £1,000 each, and putting two in one of his coat pockets and the third in another pocket, invited the gullible Wildman

to select a pocket. It did not amaze any of those who knew the sly O'Kelly that the chosen pocket only had one note in it! This transaction was a tragedy, since O'Kelly was never elected to any of the exclusive sweepstakes for which only horses owned by members of these Clubs were eligible. Lord Grosvenor once offered O'Kelly the huge price of 11,000 guineas for Eclipse, but the offer was instantly refused.

During the racing careers of

Eclipse and Highflyer revolutionary changes were occurring on the Turf, many of them being detailed in the Racing Calendars produced by John Pound, a Newmarket auctioneer, William Fawconer, William Tutin and James Weatherby, a Newcastle solicitor. There was no law of copyright and consequently a great deal of antagonism between these rivals before Weatherby gradually established his Calendar as the authentic record of the English

Right, an early photograph of the great St Simon taken at the end of the nineteenth century. He was one of the most famous racehorses of all time and was never beaten.

Below, Gladiateur stunned English racegoers in 1865 by winning the Derby and the St Leger. He was a French horse and there was no long tradition of thoroughbred breeding in France as there was in England, so the fact that a horse of his calibre had been produced so quickly in France came as a surprise.

Turf. In his Calendar he set out details of all races, and it is noticeable that the iniquitous custom of making horses carry huge burdens began to disappear before the 1790's even though in a match at York in 1788 the two horses were expected to hump a weight of thirty stone!

Until the final three decades of the Century it was the practice not to race horses until they were four or five years old, although the inauguration of the Newmarket July stakes for two year olds in 1785 became the spring board from which many similar races were derived. Many of these two year old races had the proviso that the progeny of Eclipse and Highflyer should carry three pounds extra. The prizes for such races were not always sovereigns, and at one Newmarket meeting the cost of entry for a sweepstake was 100 guineas and a hogshead of claret. As there were 17 subscribers the winning owner received an enormous amount of wine!

No change on the Turf was as revolutionary as that resulting from the founding of the Jockey Club whose power and authority steadily increased until it embraced not only Newmarket but also all other race-meetings. The Club originally met at the Star and Garter, a Pall Mall inn which was the haunt of many of the autocratic horse loving noblemen

of the era. Later the Club met at The Corner, Hyde Park, where Richard Tattersall put a room and a chef at their disposal. Eventually the Club realized the need to have their own premises at Newmarket and they established themselves there in the 1750s.

In the early days of the Club the most influential member was Sir Charles Bunbury, born in 1740, who was elected to the first Parliament of George III and represented Suffolk until 1784. He held decided views on every aspect of racing, and was remarkable in an age of brutality for never allowing either his stable lads or his jockeys to touch his horses with a whip. It was his belief that such ill treatment made horses vicious and restive and even in races he was reluctant to allow his jockeys to wear spurs. He was vehemently opposed to the customary practice of sweating horses and attempted to prevent the excessive four and five mile races which he claimed were unnecessarily severe. His passionate interest in racing was largely the cause of the disastrous failure of his marriage to the lovely Lady Sarah Lennox, whose behaviour afterwards became a *cause célébre*. His chief claims to racing fame rest upon his breeding of Highflyer, and his good fortune in owing Diomed who won the first Derby at Epsom in 1780.

Epsom had been fashionable since 1618 when the discovery of the mineral springs turned the Surrey village into a prosperous Spa. It was also considered an excellent centre for hunting, cock fighting and horse racing. In 1774 General Burgoyne sold his Epsom home called 'The Oaks' to his nephew by marriage, the young Edward Stanley, who became the 12th Earl of Derby two years later. Although only twenty one years old, Edward Stanley was rich, a member of Parliament, and the owner of countless horses. He loved gambling and thought nothing of turning the drawing room at 'The Oaks' into a cock pit as his guests wagered thousands of pounds upon the result of the mains. In 1779 he and his friends organized a race for three year old fillies which they named 'The Oaks'; as a result of its success they decided to organize a

Two horses with a beautiful action galloping down to the start. Below, is a French filly ridden by Yves Saint Martin and a likely entry for the 2000 guineas and the Oaks in 1972. Left, is a very promising two-year-old Philip of Spain, ridden by Geoff Lewis, which won the New Stakes at Royal Ascot in 1971.

race for three year old colts the following summer. Thus was the Derby founded. The winner of the first Derby on May 4th 1780 was Diomed, a strong, compact chestnut colt, who stood at Sir Charles Bunbury's stud for the next sixteen years. He was not a success as a stallion and at the age of twenty was sold for fifty guineas and exported to America where to the amazement of almost everyone he not only lived another ten years but founded a dynasty from which many of the greatest horses in American racing history are descended.

The Derby and 'The Oaks' were not the first two Classic races to be established, for three years earlier Colonel Anthony St. Leger had inaugurated the race which bears his name at Doncaster. The Two Thousand Guineas and the One Thousand Guineas at Newmarket were not founded until 1809 and 1814, but once the pattern of prestige races had been created bloodstock breeders were able to concentrate upon producing stock with the speed and stamina to win such races.

Racing in the first half of the nineteenth century was dominated by the fraud and villainy of those who flaunted the authority of the Jockey Club. Horses were doped, jockeys rode at incorrect weights, four year old horses masqueraded as three year olds, and at Cambridge Daniel Dawson was publicly hanged for poisoning Newmarket horses. That such practices gradually ceased was due not only to the new sense of

*Above, Arkle, one of the great
steeplechasers of this century taking
the water jump with Pat Taafe
up in the 1966 S.G.B. chase at
Ascot.*

*Left, Mill House, Arkle's greatest
rival when he first came on the
scene, running at Cheltenham after
Arkle's retirement.*

morality which overtook Racing England after the accession of Queen Victoria, but also to the unrelenting efforts of Lord George Bentinck, described by Disraeli as 'Lord Paramount of the Turf', and after his death in 1848 to the campaigning of Admiral Rous.

Rous, born in 1795, was virtually Dictator of Racing from the middle of the nineteenth Century until his death in 1877. A man of complete integrity he was the ultimate expert upon the Rules of Racing. In 1850 he published his book 'The Laws and Practice of Horse Racing' which contained a history of the development of the English thoroughbred, the Rules of Racing and his precise explanation and interpretation of them, the duties of racecourse officials, and a detailed list of various involved racing cases. Rous believed in the gradual improvement of the English thoroughbred during the previous century, and was convinced that the best horses of 1750 would be beaten by the worst of 1850. He also had decided ideas on handicaps which he considered 'offered a premium to fraud, for horses are constantly started without any intention of winning merely to deceive the handicapper'. In 1855 Rous was appointed handicapper to the Jockey Club and was responsible for drawing up the Weight for Age scale which is still valid. He abhorred betting, especially after his friend the Hon. Berkeley Craven shot himself as a result of his inability to settle his debts after Bay Middleton won the 1836 Derby. Bay Middleton stood 16.1½ at the time of his Epsom victory – almost 2½ inches taller than Eclipse when he raced seventy years earlier.

Ten years after Rous became handicapper English racing was stunned by the triumphs of Gladiateur in the Two Thousand Guineas, Derby and St. Leger. The fact that a French horse, owned by the son of one of Napoleon's Generals, had vanquished the best three year olds in England seemed both fantastic and almost unbelievable. Not without justification was Gladiateur hailed as 'The Avenger of Waterloo'. The real significance of Gladiateur's victories lay in the achievement of French breeders to produce a top class horse less than fifty years after the inception of French racing.

There had been little racing in France until after the Revolution and the end of the Napoleonic Wars. Curiously it was an Englishman living in Paris, Lord Henry Seymour, who gave the initial impetus to French racing. Encouraged by the heir to the throne, Ferdinand Philippe Duc d'Orleans, Seymour was responsible for founding the French Jockey Club in 1833. The original intention was that the Club should not only be exclusive socially but also the authority and arbiter on the rules and administration of racing in the vicinity of Paris. This dual purpose proved unsatisfactory and consequently a separation occurred with election to the Jockey Club becoming a highly coveted social distinction whilst the 'Societé d'encouragement pour l'amelioration des races de Chevaux en France' was created with Government support. Wisely the newly formed Society realized the futility of attempting to develop a French strain of thoroughbred independent of English bloodlines and were not averse to importing English stock upon which to establish their breeding interests. In 1837 the Prix du Jockey Club, the French equivalent to the Derby was run for the first time at Chantilly. Twenty years later racing took place at the gracious Longchamp course in the Bois de Boulogne. It is appropriate that an imposing bronze statue of Gladiateur stands at the entrance to Longchamp racecourse.

Two decades after Gladiateur's success one of the greatest of English thoroughbreds appeared on the racing scene – St Simon. St Simon's dam was an undistinguished 16 year old mare named St Angela, and it had not been considered worthwhile to enter St Simon for either the Derby or the St Leger. The young Duke of Portland bought St Simon for 1,600 guineas on the death of his breeder, Prince Batthany, and the purchase proved a bargain of the century, for St Simon was never beaten. The outstanding jockey of the era, Fred Archer, stated that St Simon was the greatest horse of all time, and less politely but enthusiastically exclaimed 'he is not a

The famous Italian racehorse Ribot winning the King George VI and Queen Elizabeth Stakes at Ascot.

horse, he's a blooming steam engine'. The Duke of Portland was a very lucky owner for he won the Derby with both Donovan and Ayrshire, but neither of these two horses were in the same class as St Simon. At the Duke's stud at Welbeck Abbey St Simon became leading sire on nine occasions, his offspring dominated the bloodstock industry for more than thirty years, and before his death at the age of twenty seven he had sired the winners of 571 races including seventeen Classics.

The most popular of these Classic triumphs came in 1896 when Persimmon who was owned by the Prince of Wales won the Derby. Four years later Diamond Jubilee, a full brother to Persimmon, won the Triple Crown for the Prince, whose third Derby victory came in 1909, by which time he was King of England. The colt who had the distinction of carrying the King's colours was Minoru, whom the King had leased from Colonel Hall Walker who was created Lord Wavertree in 1919. The latter's views on breeding were described as preposterous, inspired and eccentric but the fact remains that he bred the winner of the Gimcrack stakes at York – one of the prestige two year old races of the season – four times in five years, a feat never accomplished before or since. He has three claims to racing immortality for not only did he lease Minoru (named after the son of his Japanese gardener) to the King, but he also gave his 1,000 acre stud farm at Tully near Curragh to the nation for the purpose of founding a national stud, and introduced H H Aga Khan to English racing. Years later the Aga Khan stated 'It was entirely due to Lord Wavertree and my personal friendship with him that I started to race on the English Turf. I would probably have never been known as an owner West of Suez had he not, during and after my visit to Tully in 1904, urged me to take up racing in England . . . I never took an important decision without asking his opinion'.

Although he was forty four years of age before he began racing in Europe, H H Aga Khan had diligently read the works of leading French, English and German authorities on breeding, and had discussed their theories and opinions with the most prominent breeders on both sides of the English Channel. He was so impressed by a book published in 1902, entitled 'Croisements Rationnels dans la Race Pure' and written by a regular French cavalry officer, Colonel Vuillier, that when he began to build up his bloodstock interests in France he employed Vuillier as his manager and adviser. The Colonel, having analysed the pedigree of winning racehorses to the twelfth generation (every horse has 4,096 ancestors to this generation) concluded that certain sires were desirable in the make up of a top class racehorse. He recommended, therefore, that if a stallion was deficient in any of the required bloodlines that this should be rectified by mating the horse with one who possessed the necessary line. This theory was brilliantly employed in the Aga's racing empire and was known as Vuillier's System of Dosages.

Above, a portrait of the renowned
Arab charger which belonged to
Colonel Byerley at the end of the
seventeenth century and which was
the great grandfather of the
immortal Eclipse.

Left, Lester Piggot on Athens Wood,
the 1971 St Leger winner.

Right, Jo Mercer wearing the
Queen's colours on Albany.

Opposite page, top, foals with a great future ... a valuable Thoroughbred foal and a white Arab foal.

Centre, the Canadian bred and American owned Nijinsky with Lester Piggot up after winning the 2000 guineas at Newmarket.

Bottom, seconds after the start and they are all still bunched together.

Below, the field taking the water jump in the 1971 Grand National Steeplechase at Aintree.

Five Derby winners – Blenheim, Bahram, Mahmoud, My Love and Tulyar – and a host of other great horses won in the Aga's 'chocolate and green' silks first known to English racegoers when they saw the flying filly Mumtaz Mahal. H H Aga Khan headed the list of winning owners thirteen times and winning breeders ten times, and understandably breeders took notice when he wrote a letter to The Times in 1950 'at this moment when so many who rule the Turf and so great a part of the Press are obviously perplexed and on the look out for ways and means to keep up the prestige of the English thoroughbred, I have one piece of advice to offer – be careful when you throw out the water from the tub. Do not let the baby fall as well – and that baby is SPEED'.

During the decades when H H Aga Khan was dominating Racing a dapper chesnut colt named

Hyperion who stood only 15.1½ won the 1933 Derby in the colours of Lord Derby. No horse has had a greater impact upon the world's bloodstock industry than this colt who became Champion sire on six occasions, and whose stud record would have been even greater if it had not been for the outbreak of the Second World War. Amongst his offspring Owen Tudor, Aureole and Sun Chariot enhanced his reputation in England whilst in America Alibhai, Khaled and Heliopolis added to his fame. Hollywood film tycoon Louis B. Meyer is reputed to have offered Lord Derby a blank cheque for Hyperion, and when the offer was declined was lucky to acquire Alibhai. On the evening of Hyperion's death Lord Derby brought up from his cellar the remains of the last bottle of his most rare Napoleon brandy, and he and his guests drank to Hyperion's

Left, the great racehorse of the 1970s, Mill Reef, with Geoff Lewis up, being led into the winner's enclosure after the King George VI and Queen Elizabeth Stakes at Ascot.

Right, Horses and jockeys straining every muscle as they near the finishing post.

memory. The bottle had been opened for a visit of Sir Winston
Churchill, and at a later date Lord
Derby declared 'I still have the
bottle in a glass case outside my
Estate Office alongside other family
treasures. After all it had been used
to pay tribute to the two greatest
G.O.M's of our time'.

Hyperion was inbred to St Simon
as were Nearco and Ribot, the two
other world famous horses who
influenced Racing before the era of
Sea Bird, Vaguely Noble and
Nijinsky. Both Nearco and Ribot
were bred by Signor Federico Tesio,
a man of immense talent who was a
scholar, an amateur jockey, a painter,
an architect and an authority on
bloodstock breeding. In 1898 he
founded a stud at Dormello on the
shores of Lake Maggiore. The
essence of his method of improving
Italian bloodstock was to purchase
English bred fillies and mate them
with the best European stallions.
Although racing had flourished at
Naples, Florence, Milan and Rome
for 50 years, and King Vittorio
Emmanuele II had imported English

bloodstock in his enthusiasm to
improve Italian thoroughbreds, it
was Tesio who was responsible for
the Italian challenge to the
supremacy of English and French
racing.

In 1911 he bred the first of his
twenty-one Italian Derby winners –
winners which included Donatello
II, Niccolo dell Arca, Nearco,
Tenerani and Ribot. After Nearco
had won the Italian Derby he
triumphed in the Grand Prix de
Paris where his defeated rivals included Bois Roussel, winner of the
English Derby, and Cillas, winner
of the French Derby. He was sold
by Tesio to Mr Martin Benson for
the record sum of £60,000. Sent to
Benson's stud at Newmarket he
became an immense influence on
world bloodstock, for in addition to
siring the English Classic winners
Dante, Nimbus, Sayajirao, Masaka
and Neasham Belle, he sired Moss-
borough, Royal Charger and the
brilliant but temperamental Nas-
rullah who became Champion sire
in the United States. Ribot ex-
emplified Tesio's astuteness in

breeding from horses acquired
cheaply, for one of his great grand
dams was bought at the Doncaster
sales for 140 guineas, and one of his
grand dams at the Newmarket sales
for 350 guineas. Not bad bargains
when it is remembered that Ribot
won the Prix de l'Arc de Triomphe
twice before going to stud and siring
Molvedo, Ragusa, Tom Rolfe, Arts
and Letters and Graustark.

Racing today is international, and
the facts that three of the past four
Epsom Derby winners were bred in
North America, and the sires of the
past three Oaks heroines exported to
Japan, speak for themselves.
Volumes have been written giving
advice on the subject of the breeding
of thoroughbreds from the econo-
mic, veterinary and historical point
of view, but without the essential
ingredient of 'good luck' success will
prove elusive no matter how carefully the advice is followed. Yet
for those who are so clever or
fortunate as to breed and train an
Eclipse, a St Simon, Hyperion or
Nearco, life on earth is a very
heaven.

Thoroughbred racing in America

WALTER D OSBORNE

It is almost impossible to compare the Thoroughbred Industry in the United States with that in any other part of the world where racing is conducted, because American racing is conducted on a much larger scale than anywhere else. To begin with, more than half of all the Thoroughbred horses in the world are foaled in the United States. And even this is hardly enough to supply the demands of over one hundred race tracks, many of which conduct meetings that last for months on end. (In States like New York, New Jersey, and Maryland, there is hardly a 'dark day' in the year-around racing calendar.) A conservative estimate has placed the value of the American Thoroughbred establishment, including breeding farms, livestock, and race courses, at a total of three billion dollars – a figure that cannot be matched anywhere in the entire world of sports. Racing in America has an annual attendance of more than forty million fans, who bet some three and a half billion dollars in the course of a year. United States Thoroughbred race tracks return nearly $300 million to the states in tax revenue. The sport, moreover, gives direct employment to more than 60,000 people.

Yet this sheer size does not necessarily mean that American racing, in the overall picture, is also the best to be found anywhere. It is true to say that the top breeders and stable owners in the United States produce and race animals of a quality comparable to any that can be found in the British Isles or on the European continent. Thoroughbreds of American, or predominantly American, bloodlines have competed successfully in many of the richest overseas stakes events, and such well-known American bloodlines as those established by Fair Play (sire of the great Man o' War), Domino, and Ben Brush, can be found in the pedigrees of many of the finest race horses foaled on foreign soil.

In the United States the top calibre Thoroughbreds compete for purses in the hundred-thousand dollar and over category at 'classic' distances of from a mile and a half to two miles, the sort of events in which a champion horse is truly tested. But the number of these 'stayers', horses of great heart and stamina, is but a drop in the bucket when contrasted with the huge number of sprinters, animals capable of only a mile or less, that are foaled in this country.

The reason for this is, as horsemen know, that it is far more predictable to breed for short speed than it is for stamina over the longer routes. The insatiable demands of American race tracks for more animals have resulted in an increasing production of these so–called 'speed horses'. At many of the lesser tracks days may pass before an event is scheduled for more than a mile.

Dr Fager winning at Aqueduct in his final race in 1969.

100

Even at the major tracks on the East Coast in Florida and California, most of the contests on a nine-race card will be at sprint distances of from less than six up to seven and a half furlongs, or a mile at most. Thus, while American breeders do indeed produce some of the world's greatest Thoroughbreds, their ratio to the total annual crop is without question lower than it is in England, Ireland or France. And to maintain the sort of quality that is still a requirement of the more exacting American stable owners, it has often been necessary to go abroad and import outstanding stallions like the Franco-Italian Ribot, and the great French champion Seabird, as well as broodmares with pedigrees indicative of fine stamina qualities.

Horse racing of one sort or another has been a part of the American scene almost since the establishment of the very first British colonies in the Maryland-Virginia tidewater country in the early years of the seventeenth century. The first horse races on American soil were held on the rutted dirt streets of the colonial towns. (To this day, many of the older towns in this part of the country still have long, straight thoroughfares called 'race street'.) As the settlements became more civilized, street racing was banned as too dangerous to pedestrians and the racing people took their sport to the countryside. At this time the tidewater country was heavily forested, and to conduct their racing contests the sportsmen of the day hacked out narrow straightways through the woods. These were generally about a quarter of a mile in length and were known as 'quarter paths'.

During the middle and latter years of the century, the prosperous planters of Virginia, Maryland, and a bit later South Carolina, began importing 'horses of the blood' from England. Unfortunately, these fine horses were wholly unsuited to the mad pace of the quarter mile race paths, in which horses were sent off from a rearing, plunging start, at the tap of the drum or musket shot, in a wild sort of dash toward the end post a few hundred yards

The first formal race meeting in America took place in 1665 on the Hempstead Plains of Long Island near what is now Garden City.

102

away. The good quality imports could barely get into stride before the race was over. However, the colonists made the happy discovery that, by crossing their better English horses with the tough little Chickasaw ponies they acquired mostly by barter with the Indians, they could develop a strain of animals with the blinding take-off speed their sport demanded and which also were highly durable working horses in the everyday work of the plantation. However, this breed of horses began to fall out of favour around 1700, as more land was cleared and fields were staked out for longer 'end to end', English-style contests. Eventually, they found their way into the American West, where they gained new popularity as being the best-suited of any breed in the qualities of agility, ruggedness, and 'stock sense', needed by the cowboys to handle the huge, unruly longhorn cattle bands that roamed the western plains. They are perpetuated to this day in the American Quarter Horse family – by far the largest registered breed of horse in the United States.

While the planter aristocracy of the south-east undoubtedly had the best racing blood in the colonies during the pre-revolutionary days, it was not here that the first formal race track was laid out. That distinction belongs to New York. The exact location of this original American race course is not known, but it 'was at a place then called Salisbury Plain, in the general vicinity of Garden City, Long Island, not far from the site of modern Belmont Park. Founder of this track was Colonel Richard Nicolls, colonial Governor of New York. Opened in 1665, it was called Newmarket, after the famous race course established in England by Charles II.

The War of the American Revolution was fought mainly in rather dense and rugged countryside, unsuited for major cavalry movements (which was a very good thing for the rebelling colonists since England, at that time, possessed mounted troops second to none in the world). Nevertheless, the war did disrupt to a considerable extent

A print of Peytona and Fashion in their great match for $20,000 over the Union course in 1845. Peytona won and this was the last of the great North-South clashes in the years before the Civil War.

the breeding and racing of blooded horses which had become very well established in most of the colonies by the time the conflict began. In fact, a number of the leading American revolutionary figures, among them George Washington and Thomas Jefferson, were prominent in racing circles in the years just prior to the war.

After hostilities ceased, the citizens of the new nation were not slow in getting racing back on its feet. Between the years 1784 and 1798, four English stallions were imported

from England and from these sires were developed bloodlines, not only of great importance in early American Thoroughbred breeding, but still to be found in the pedigrees of many of the best American horses. They were, in order, Medley, a smallish but handsome son of the famous British Gimcrack; Shark, a brown horse by Marske, an animal which had been highly successful in English racing; Messenger, by Mambrino, who was destined to become the founding father of the American harness racing family as

Above, Man O' War working out. He was only defeated once in twenty one starts.

Top right, mares and foals graze quietly at a celebrated stud farm in the Kentucky blue grass region.

Right, passing the stands for the first time in a mile-and-a-half event at Old Saratoga.

105

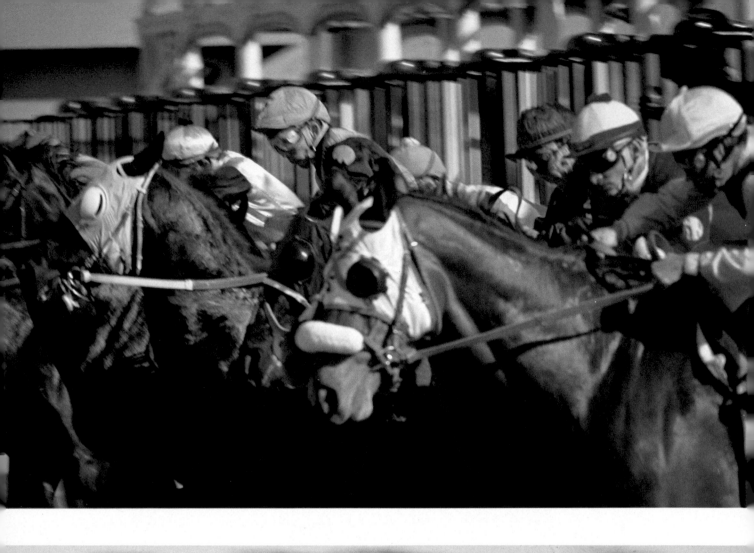

Left, the jockeys give their horses their heads on leaving the starting gates but shorten rein and start to balance their horses as soon as they can after the start.

Below left, jockeys ask their mounts for that last ounce of reserve as they drive toward the end pole at Delaware Park, near Willington, Delaware.

Right, a pair of thoroughbreds working out together at Saratoga's 'Oklahoma' training track.

Below, a jockey brings his horse to the front as the field pass the stands for the first time at Aqueduct.

Right, the great Kelso – history's leading money winner setting out for morning exercise accompanied by his trainer.

Left, two handsome stable mates being given their early morning exercise.

Below, horses coming down the back stretch at Saratoga.

well as a notable sire of Thorough-breds, and finally the winner of the first Epsom Derby, Diomed. Some-how, Diomed had while at stud in England acquired a bad reputation as a breeder and he was bought from a dealer by the Virginian sportsman, John Hoomes, for 250. Diomed was twenty-one years of age at the time he reached American shores but almost instantly he proved to be a most successful sire. Bred to a mare belonging to Hoomes' friend and business asso-ciate John Tayloe, Diomed sired, among other good American horses, the famous Sir Archy, destined in turn to become the greatest race horse and stallion that had been foaled in the United States up until that time.

During his racing career, Sir Archy campaigned in the silks of William Ransom Johnson, who had purchased him from Tayloe. John-son, a native of North Carolina,

was by far the most influential figure in American racing circles during the early years of the new republic, so much so that it usually came as a big surprise when one of his horses lost a race. (There was, in fact, a period of two years – 1807 and 1808 – when Johnson's race horses only failed to win in two out of sixty-three contests.)

As time passed, American breeders 'went back to the well' for new infusions of English blood. Unquestionably the British stallion who would in short order establish himself as the best of these later imports was Glencoe, purchased by the Irish born Tennesseean, James Jackson, in 1838. For eight years, Glencoe was the leading sire of American winners. One of these was the filly Peytona, whose win-nings set a new American record for her sex.

During the early Federal years, the South – most notably Virginia

and Maryland – was the hub of both breeding and racing. But it wasn't long before the sport became popular around the big northern cities, particularly New York. A sort of sporting rivalry between North and South began in 1823 when William Ransom Johnson named Sir Henry, a son of Sir Archy, to compete in a match race against the northern horse, American Eclipse, belonging to the New York sportsman, Cornelius van Ranst, at New York's Union Race Course. American Eclipse won this encounter but in 1836 Johnson sent John Bascombe to challenge van Ranst's Post Boy and got his revenge. In 1842, Johnson returned to New York with his very successful nine-year-old Boston and was unexpectedly defeated by the New Jersey bred mare Fashion. The last of these North–South clashes in the years before the Civil War came in 1845 when Glencoe's great daughter, Peytona, was shipped to Union Race Course to take the measure of that same Fashion in two hotly contested heats. (The practice

of racing in two or more heats, sometimes as long as four miles each, was perpetuated in the United States long after it had gone out of style in England.)

During the years leading up to the American Civil War, racing had expanded rapidly in the United States. Race tracks, originally no more than an oval racing strip enclosed by rails, had become more elaborate. Stands were erected, concessionaires set up shop to cater for the growing number of patrons, and public betting through bookmakers now began operating.

At the close of the pre-Civil War period, there were major centres of racing at New York, Baltimore, Chicago, Cincinnati, New Orleans, Charleston, and St Louis. In California, several small tracks were flourishing in the wake of the great gold rush. None of these resembled the truly palatial race courses of years to come, but Thoroughbred racing had definitely come in from the country to become the big city spectator attraction that it is in the United States today.

The war years virtually wiped out the old breeding establishments in the tidewater country, and after the war was over the focus was increasingly on Kentucky, which had been spared much of the conflict's devastation, and where a number of the old Virginia breeders had already established themselves even before hostilities commenced. (Kentucky still leads the nation both in the quality and quantity of Thoroughbreds raised there, although California, Florida, and Maryland are increasing in stature every year – the most remarkable growth having been in the Ocala, Florida area.)

Racing, too, during the war years, was conducted on a very reduced scale. But as soon as the war ended it staged a big return – too big, as it turned out. Even while hostilities were drawing to a close in 1864, famous Old Saratoga opened its gates for the first time, and in the decade immediately following peace, three other major racing centres were inaugurated. These were Pimlico, at Baltimore, in 1870; the Fair

Racing at Hialeah Park, Florida.

Grounds, at New Orleans, in 1872; and Churchill Downs, at Louisville, in 1875. All four tracks are still popular race courses to this day, with Churchill Downs, of course, drawing the attention of the entire racing world as the scene of the annual Kentucky Derby for three-year-olds, America's most famous horse race.

At the same time, racing in the Old South, once so popular in states like Georgia, Alabama, Tennessee, Virginia and the Carolinas, wilted in the years following the Civil War before the onslaught of new moralistic religious sects. Only in Maryland and Louisiana, where the more tolerant Roman Catholic tradition prevailed, was southern racing perpetuated. (Many years later it also took strong roots in Florida, today the scene of some of the most important winter racing.)

The immediate post-Civil War years also saw the abandonment of the old method of racing in long punishing heats. The jockey, who in earlier years was quite often an obscure and minor actor in the drama of racing, began coming to the fore as a sort of popular folk hero, or villain, depending on how he fared. Development of the so-called American 'racing seat', the low, forward crouch with the rider's weight balanced over the horse's withers, began around this time. Later, it was introduced into England by the great American jockeys Tod Sloan and Danny Maher, who rode for Edward, Prince of Wales and Lord Rosebery respectively, and with such success that British jockeys soon abandoned their straight up-in-the-saddle riding technique in favour of the style which they originally had derided as 'the monkey on a stick' seat.

Powerful Jim McLaughlin, hard-whipping Fred Taral, and the exciting Edward 'Snapper' Garrison, who liked to come from behind in a blazing finish drive, were among the leading American jockeys in the years between the Civil War and the turn of the twentieth century. (Garrison's heart-stopping finishing tactics, like those of the Chifneys in England, gave rise to a still popular American racing term, the 'Garrison finish', the equivalent of the 'Chifney Rush', in British turf terminology.)

Together with Tod Sloan, as brilliant on the American track as he was in England, the other greatest rider of the period was gentle-mannered Isaac 'Ike' Murphy. One of the many well-known black riders of that day, Murphy won on an amazing 44 per cent of the 1,400 mounts he accepted – a record not approached by any other jockey in the world since Murphy's time. Murphy made a great deal of money in his day, though he is known to have given a good deal of it away to poorer friends and relatives. But he never had the opportunity to enjoy it at leisure, dying of pneumonia soon after he retired at the age of 37.

It was in the same years that many of American racing's most important fixtures were first run. The Travers, the United States' oldest stakes event, was first contested at Saratoga in 1864, where it is still run, when that track opened in the waning war years. The three

Above, many racehorses in America wear blinkers for protection on the dirt tracks. These also serve the additional purpose of keeping the horses' minds on the job as they are raced very frequently.

Left, the final spurt round the corner at Delmar, California.

so-called 'triple crown' races were inaugurated soon after with the oldest of these events, the Belmont Stakes, first run in 1867. The Preakness, at Pimlico, followed in 1873 and two years later, the Kentucky Derby had its initial running. Maryland's Dixie Handicap and New York's Jerome Stakes for three-year-olds, were among other major American racing events which originated in the immediate post-war years.

Many were the great horses that made their mark on the American turf during the years between 1865 and 1900 – the fleet filly Ruthless, winner of the inaugural Belmont Stakes; unbeaten Norfolk; and the mighty Longfellow, who came out of Kentucky to thrash the northerner, Harry Basset, in a post-war renewal of the old North–South rivalry, held in 1872 at New Jersey's Monmouth Park. (Two weeks later, Harry Basset returned the favour by beating Longfellow at Saratoga.) It was during the latter part of this period that important native American Thoroughbred families were

established by Hanover, Domino and Ben Brush, names which still have a special lustre in the pedigrees of the best Thoroughbreds, both in the United States and abroad.

The growth of racing in the United States in the interval between the Civil War and World War 1, reached unchecked, epidemic proportions toward the close of the century. While the entire era was graced by such fine animals and good racing that it is still referred to as the 'golden age' of American racing, it was also a time when many abuses crept into the sport in the form of doping animals, fixing races, and introducing ringers – horses racing under other names than their own. As these irregularities became more and more flagrant and therefore more widely publicized, a storm of public indignation rose against the entire Thoroughbred sport. Not all of this was justified. But there was sufficient tangible evidence of wrong-doing to bring on a wave of anti-racing legislation that was so repressive that, by the time the first decade of the new century had

113

The field pounds up the track away from the gates at Saratoga, New York.

ended, racing in the United States was continued in only two states, Maryland and Kentucky. Many of the big stables had taken their horses abroad or to Canada to race. A Jockey Club, similar to that in England, had been organized back in 1894 to try to check the evil practices that had invaded racing to the point where the sport's very existence was threatened. Many of the members of this organization would, after Thoroughbred racing regained respectability in the mind of the public, play important roles in seeing that its progress followed more orderly lines in the future. But for the time being, their voices were lost in the tumult of public outrage.

The story of how racing in the

United States started its painful comeback goes back to the 1908 running of the Kentucky Derby. At this time the city fathers in Louisville were also feeling some of the anti-racing pressure that had been so effective elsewhere. An obscure 'blue law', which forbade trackside book-making, was suddenly brought to light and the city government announced that it would be enforced. Matt Winn, the resourceful ex-tailor who was then running Churchill Downs, had an answer – one which in time would solve many problems for racing everywhere. He had, some years previously, bought several French totalisator machines, devices through which the public establishes

its own odds according to the various amounts bet on each horse in a race. Winn had tried this out before, but it had been a flop with the betting public who preferred shopping around for the best odds with the bookmakers. With no competition from the chalk men, however, the pari-mutuel machines proved popular with the fans. Not only was the Derby saved but also, in many ways, was all racing in the United States.

Trying to tax racing revenue by some control over the human bookmakers was a difficult – sometimes impossible – task. But with the mechanical odds-makers recording each sum wagered, it was not hard for the lawmakers to perceive that a

regular percentage could be deducted from each betting pool, in return for licensing the sport, and, in this way, produce a lucrative amount of state revenue. Also, with pari-mutuel style betting, it was made considerably more difficult for big time gamblers to pull off huge betting coups, one of the abuses that had led to racing's downfall.

Through the pari-mutuels and the vigilance of new state racing commissions established to police the sport, racing in America was rapidly restored at the major Thoroughbred centres and in a form so free of criminal taint that it is considered by many people to be the cleanest of all big time

sports in the United States.

While much American racing in modern times has been forced, by an ever-increasing demand for race horses, to go the route of cheap sprinters, it would be patently unfair not to point out that the entire period, from the end of World War I to the present day, has been graced by some of the finest race horses ever bred in any part of the world. This epoch has seen the likes of Regret, the only filly ever to win the Kentucky Derby; Zev, who took the measure of the Epsom Derby winner Papyrus in a special match race at Belmont Park; triple crown winners Sir Barton, Gallant Fox, Omaha, War Admiral, Whirlaway, Count Fleet, Assault and

Citation, and many other stout campaigners. Greater perhaps than even any of these, was Samuel Riddle's immortal Man O' War, defeated in only one of twenty-one starts – and that time through bad racing luck. Mention too must be made of Willis Sharpe Kilmer's tough old gelding Exterminator who, in an amazing eight-year career, won fifty out of a hundred starts.

The more recent years have seen other superb American Thoroughbreds go to the post: Bold Ruler, Swaps, Nashua, Round Table, Native Dancer, Stymie, Tom Fool, Buckpasser, Damascus, Dr Fager, Arts and Letters and, of course, Kelso, leading money winner in history and one of racing's true all-time 'greats', – a clear indication that while much American racing, in the overall, does suffer from some lack of 'class', the upper echelon of the breeding establishment in the United States is still quite capable of turning out top quality animals. There is every reason that it will continue to do so as long as there remain owners in racing whose dedication to the sport transcends their desire for a quick dollar.

There have never been men more knowledgeable in the training and riding of Thoroughbred race horses than there have in the past half century, that period of time in which American racing staged its impressive return from near oblivion. American racing justly honours such fine trainers as James 'Sunny Jim' Fitzsimmons, Max Hirsch, and Hirsch Jacobs, the most successful trainer of all time. All three of these recently deceased conditioners had careers which spanned the greater part of the whole period. Since then, younger men have been coming along rapidly to continue in the same tradition: trainers like Elliott Burch, Jim Maloney, Johnny Nerud, and Eddie Neloy, whose untimely death in 1971 ended a truly meteoric career.

The justly deserved reputation of American race riders – the spiritual heirs of the nineteenth century pioneers who taught the rest of the world how to ride race horses – has also never been better than in these past five decades which have witnessed the riding feats of Earl

Sande, Johnny Loftus, John Longden, George Woolf, George Edward 'Eddie' Arcaro, Ted Atkinson, William Shoemaker, to whose numbers, in recent years, must be added the names of such fine Latin American riders as Braulio Baeza, Manuel Ycaza, Eddie Belmonte, Angel Cordero and numerous other visitors from south of the border.

In a word, American Thoroughbred racing, though it must make concessions to fill race cards for many unimportant events, still has the men and horses to provide a goodly amount of top quality sport in major stakes events.

Two beautiful heads of horses: above a 1971 leading filly who has just won her race and will go to stud next year, and right, the American-owned Nijinsky who raced so well in the 1970s in Britain and is now at stud in America.

116

Pony clubs and riding clubs

JUDITH CAMPBELL

To the uninitiated the words 'Pony Club' can conjure up a vision of a crowd of little girls with 'jockey caps' tilted snootily over their noses, tittuping their ponies around a Colonel Blimpish figure as he bellows out the quasi-military commands of out-dated riding instruction. The truth is somewhat different.

The Pony Club stands for many different things to many different people. It can be the heavensent answer to the prayers of hopelessly un-horseminded parents saddled with pony-mad children. It CAN provide the solution to the apparently devilish pony that plays up and takes off at the mere sight of another of its own species. It has proved itself many times over to be an excellent nursery for the future top class performer, often at International level. But above all the Pony Club still provides an enormous amount of fun and interest for thousands of young people under 21 living in many different countries.

Up to the First World War horses and ponies were everywhere still very much part of everyday life, and most of the families who possessed them as a matter of course had ingrained, inherited horse-sense and usually a family groom. Then came the stringencies of the war years, and afterwards the machine age rapidly took over, until owning a horse or pony was a rare luxury and several generations grew up mostly

without any basic horse knowledge or interest. This state of affairs did not necessarily stop children from wanting to ride, but it did provide their parents with good reason for not doing anything about it. And too often where they complied and a pony joined the family, sheer lack of 'know how' resulted in a frightened child put off riding for ever, or a spoilt pony being sold downhill through no fault of its own, or even cases of unintentional cruelty. Now, largely owing to the good work of the Pony Club all over the world such instances are rare, and the pleasures of riding and the real needs of horses and ponies are yearly becoming better known.

The Pony Club in Britain began life in 1929, when an offshoot of what was then the British Institute of the Horse was welded into an association to encourage children to ride, to enjoy the sports and pastimes connected with horses and ponies, and to learn how to look after their own animals. From the very beginning the idea was popular. By 1934 there were 8,000 members, and the numbers increased rapidly until the outbreak of World War II closed all Branches for the next six years. It was an act of faith to start up again in 1945, since a revival of widespread general interest in riding and ponies appeared remote at a time when the attention of both young and old was fixed on machines and television, and the

Two friends await their daily exercise.

Left, a keen pony being taken over a home-made fence in the hedge by his young rider.

Right, the author's daughter with her pony.

actuality of space-travel was only round the corner. But it turned out that children still wanted to be involved with living creatures, that learning to care for ponies did interest them, and that the lure of the countryside remained irresistible. The present and still growing total Pony Club membership of 80,000 proves the point.

The backbone of the Pony Club has always been the working rally. These meetings are usually held in the Easter and Summer holidays, but in Canada some of the Branches reverse the order, and if a heated, indoor school is available they confine their Club activities to the cold winter months. But whether a rally is being held under the cloudless skies of an Australian summer, or at 6.30 a.m. in the already steamy heat of Singapore, or in the steady downpour of what should be a

flaming August day in England, the programme is much the same.

The chief business at a rally is instructions in riding and jumping at different levels, and in the care of pony and 'tack'. The members are divided into groups, or 'rides' according to their ability, and the child who rides her rough pony well will go into a more senior ride than the perfectly accoutred child with a show pony, who is less able. Even the most nervous novice is sure to find others of the same standard, and the bottom ride often contains quite young children – although here the help of an active teenager on foot, with a leading rein to act as handbrake, can be very useful.

Nowadays a big effort is made to keep all instruction in line and up to date, but the teaching is flexible and suited to the particular needs of different clubs. In Canada for in-

stance there are several that cater exclusively for the members who prefer to ride 'Western', in the relaxed style of the cowboy, rather than in the more conventional 'English' position, and the lower grades of the Pony Club tests are modified accordingly. A Rally is not all work and time is given to having fun and to the joy of 'just riding' when children play mounted games and go for the occasional country ride, at the same time learning Country Lore which is part of the curriculum.

Pony Club officials, of whom the majority offer their services for free, do the coaching and examining for the various Pony Club Tests and train aspirants to a team for one of the Inter-Branch competitions. They are also always willing to advise on such matters as the most suitable bit for a particular pony, or to point out tactfully why a saddle like the 'Pony Club Approved' is likely to do more for the rider's position than Dad's pre-war ex-hunting saddle. They will do their best to find a remedy for the foibles of a problem pony, but reserve the right to turn away any animal that appears a real danger to its own or other rides, or any mares in foal, the occasional one that comes complete with foal 'at foot', and any that are too infirm, too young or too aged for the job.

Obviously to have his own pony is every member's ambition, but it is not a requisite for joining the Pony Club. Many of the ponies attending rallies are hired for the occasion, and in towns where restricted space sometimes necessitates instructing Rides in turn, the same pony often copes with two riders. Most Clubs also include a few dismounted rallies during the year, used for demonstrating such important items as feeding or shoeing, or for paying a visit to some place of interest like a racing stud or Hunt Kennels.

The Pony Club does its best to cater for most riding tastes. The athletic horse vaulting is very popular with boy members in the States, and is an American Pony Club speciality; polo lessons and matches are also very well attended and organized by many Branches. In Britain there is a Senior and Junior annual Polo Tournament, and an exclusively masculine sport is Pen-tathlon championships, which include tests in running, fencing, shooting and swimming as well as in riding.

Eventing, the prevalent name for Horse Trials, is an increasingly popular sport in many countries, and at Pony Club level helps to further the exciting scheme for members to exchange visits, not only to other Branches at home but also overseas. Horse Trials consist of three phases, Dressage, Cross Country, and Show Jumping, and there are Inter-Branch Team competitions as well as international competitions. The Inter-Territorial Horse Trials, put on by the thriving South African Pony Clubs, usually include teams from Britain and

Left, the Pony Club doesn't mind how young the pupils are . . .

Below, it must be the ambition of many Pony Club members who enjoy show jumping to own a horse like this . . . Beethoven with his famous owner David Broome.

Rhodesia, and British members have competed in Denmark. In 1965 a team had the luck to be the first from Britain to take part in one of the International Pony Club Exchange visits, held that year in America. And although transport, even for Inter-Branch and Inter-Regional competitions is often a problem in a country as large as Canada, a Canadian team is always included in the annual Inter-Pacific Exchange with New Zealand, Australia, Japan, Britain and the USA.

As well as the Horse Trials, several Clubs have given the Show Jumping enthusiasts an annual Inter-Branch Team competition of their own as well as the Horse Trials. In 1957 Prince Philip presented a

special Challenge Cup which is named after him to the British Pony Club, and inaugurated a competition for those members up to 16 years old who ride the well-trained but non-specialist type of pony. Every year since then, teams from all over the British Isles have competed for the Pony Club Mounted Games Championship, and the winners of the area competitions ride off against each other in the thrilling finals which are part of the Horse of the Year Show in the autumn.

Some people consider that nowadays the Pony Club tends to concentrate on training the lucky few who 'make' the teams for the various competitions, at the expense of the less expert majority. In a few

cases this may be true, but this is a competitive age, and the ambition to get into a team acts as a powerful and worthwhile incentive. Also, most Branches hold their own gymkhana, Hunter Trial or even Horse Trials, geared to suit most riding standards and types of pony; and Trail Riding, open to all, is quickly becoming as favourite a pastime elsewhere as it is with the American and Canadian Clubs.

A camp is often the highlight of the Pony Club year, although few Branches can aspire to anything as wonderful as the safaris, sometimes 13,000 feet up to the snowline on Mount Kenya, enjoyed by the lucky members of the Molo Hunt and Kipkabus Pony Clubs. Nor are the

facilities of iced water and air conditioning with comparable comforts for the ponies, that are supplied by the Singapore Turf Club for their local Pony Club, usual components of camp life. But equal fun is usually had by all, whether in tents, with ponies tethered Army fashion, or in the lofts and stabling attached to some historic castle.

Branch and Club interests vary from region to region as well as in different countries, and are often determined by local conditions. A well-to-do district often means a bigger percentage of better class ponies, with the emphasis on Eventing. Built-up areas can mean confining the Club's activities within the four walls of a covered school.

Above, children learning about balance at a Pony Club rally.

Right, out to graze in a rich green field on a peaceful summer's evening.

Above, at the end of the day some
of the junior members of a country
pony club feed their ponies before
turning them loose to graze in
the field.

Right, two loveable creatures, one
from Norway (top) and one from
the Lake District.

Left, a beautifully marked Skewbald or Paint Horse.

Right, a young rider at an Australian pony club trying to fathom the mysteries of girths while his pony waits patiently.

Difficult riding terrain like that of Malta may mean that there is adequate space within some venue like that of the Marsa, the island's general sports' arena, but little change of scene. The interests of the Irish Pony Clubs reflect the traditional enthusiasm for hunting in Ireland, as do those in Cyprus, where the members quickly pass their 'C' Test in order to qualify for hunting with the Dhekelia Draghounds. Danish children are so afraid of losing any time that could possibly be spent in actual riding, that their Pony Club instructors find it difficult to instil horsemastership as well as horsemanship.

When the Pony Club was first formed in Britain practically all children rode ponies, and though nowadays a number of members take to horses at quite an early age because of the increasingly high standard of the competitions, the British Isles remain basically pony minded and the Club is certainly not mis-named. In America the opposite is true, it is only comparatively recently that Americans have given thought to ponies at all, and the Pony Clubs are not in the least height or type conscious. The majority ride horses as a matter of course, and the members' aim as expressed by the Club demonstrate how unheight-minded they are: 'To be thoroughly happy, comfortable horsemen, riding across natural country with complete confidence

A very handsome show pony with his mind on lunch . . .

and perfect balance, on a pony equally happy and free from pain or bewilderment.'

As in the States and Canada, it has been customary in Australia to pass down the ex-racehorse or stock horse to the children. A number do ride the utility types over 14 hands and under 15 hands known as Galloways, and in the Western States particularly the younger members often have strains of those active, if plain little ponies whose ancestors were imported from Timor during the nineteenth century. But it was, and in many cases still is, a common sight to see the largest component of an Australian Pony Club rally made up of quite small children perched on enormous horses! However, with the many studs of imported pony breeds, and those of the registered 'Australian Ponies' that derive from early importations of riding types, an in-

creasing number of children are using the smaller animals, and the trend is being fostered by the big variety of showing classes for ponies of different breeds and abilities.

Australia is such an enormous country that the Pony Clubs differ as much in interests as in saddlery and riding clothes. Around cities such as Melbourne the Clubs are very smart and the emphasis is on Eventing and kindred sports. The standard in dressage and jumping is good, and the Inter-Branch Horse Trials Championships have grown to a large two-day affair, with 40–50 teams competing. Both the Melbourne and Oaklands Hunts hold special Meets for children.

Up country the rallies provide enjoyable meetings for both parents and children living in scattered communities. At those gatherings the tack often consists of scaled-down stock saddles with sacks for saddle-cloths, and though members wear the obligatory hard riding-cap, the rest of their riding attire is predominantly jeans, with a wonderfully colourful assortment of jackets. The effect may not be as technically correct as that of some Pony Clubs, but the spirit is every bit as keen and the enjoyment as great. So long as safety, and comfort for the pony are not contravened, no one minds if the bridle is tied up with string, if it is done so adequately. No child is made to feel inferior, and those owning the most primitive tack can often be awarded good points for keeping it clean and supple.

Many Clubs ride on expeditions into the Australian Alps, or go from property to property spending a night at each, their ponies often accommodated and hay fed in the sheepyards. On Summer camps the boys usually sleep in the station woolshed, the girls in the shearers'

huts; the shearers' kitchen makes the perfect Mess Room, and somewhere to swim, be it river, hole, dam or pool, is an essential for after-work hours.

All members are gymkhana minded, and some Clubs play polo . . . at all levels. Most children do well at some aspect of this game, and when a Shetland, taking advantake of its rider's two-handed grip of the polo stick, dropped its head to have a snack, the language of its youthful owner would have done justice to any 10-goal player!

In October 1944 a momentous meeting at Hawkes Bay, in New Zealand's North Island, resulted in the formation of the Heretaunga Pony Club. This was the first of its kind in the Islands, and provided the prototype for the New Zealand Pony Clubs Association, which now has around 77 Branches with an approximate membership of 8,000.

Below, a very professional duo performing at Pony Club championships.

131

There was never any lack of membership material, since petrol was still rationed and many country children rode their ponies to school as a matter of course, and in the towns there were numberless children clamouring to ride who did not have the facilities to do so. An initial problem of the Pony Club was, however, to introduce and establish more modern methods of riding which were very different from those that had prevailed before. It was plain that dressage would be of small interest to the young Maori who rode miles to a rally bareback, controlling his mount with a single rope attached to part of a halter. On the other hand the children who found it easier to win gymkhana races once they had learned largely to control their ponies with seat and legs, instead of by yanking at the bit, quickly came to appreciate the value of what they were being taught. They continued to attend rallies in increasing numbers, and the whole project was helped along by the co-operation of New Zealand's numerous and influential Hunt Clubs.

The Pony Club is going from strength to strength in the Islands, and now many members are helping with a very worthwhile project for aiding disabled children by lending them their most suitable ponies to ride. This idea is gaining ground all over the world and bringing great pleasure, and proved therepeutic benefit, to many of the mentally and physically handicapped.

Riding clubs

In many ways a riding club is the adult equivalent of the Pony Club and there are numerous riding and saddle clubs in almost every country. In Britain 'The Riding Clubs' usually refers to that association of nearly three hundred clubs that includes Dressage Groups, clubs at Universities, the Saddle Clubs of the three Services, and Clubs in Jersey, Guernsey, the Isle of Man, Isle of Wight and a few overseas that are all affiliated to the British Horse Society.

The first of the Committees formed to administer this association was constituted in 1952, and

headquarters now operate from the National Equestrian Centre at Kenilworth, in Warwickshire. They keep in touch with all the various Clubs spread throughout England, Scotland and Wales, through nineteen Liaison Committees, which have the additional function of promoting co-operation between the Clubs in a particular area. Some of the Clubs have junior members who may take the Pony Club Tests if they wish by special arrangement, though they are barred from any of the official Riding Clubs' competitions until the age of seventeen.

In the early years the Riding Clubs had the reputation of being an association for 'weekend riders' only. It is perfectly correct that the membership consists largely of those who work for their living and have therefore to restrict their riding activities, but the slightly derogatory implication that the Clubs were composed only of complete novices is far from true. Nowadays the Association prides itself on having a membership that includes every kind of rider from the complete beginner to the most professional, and welcomes anyone who can ride, at whatever level, so long as they are genuinely interested in horses and equitation. The Clubs also aim to give encouragement and assistance to their members, with the wider targets of improving the overall standard in riding and horsemanship, and of preserving and developing public riding facilities.

Obviously Club activities vary but there is a flourishing social side, largely for those in urban areas, while those in country districts are more likely to have the resources for supplying instructors and for organizing competitions and the like.

Since the majority of the members have full-time jobs, many of the instructional classes and practice rides are arranged for one or two evenings a week, usually at some suitable and conveniently placed riding school. Other activities and most of the competitions take place at weekends. Many members hire horses for Club events, and some riding schools will co-operate with reduced fees for a regular arrange-

ment. Those who have their own animal often keep it at grass, because they have neither the time for daily excercising nor, possibly, the cash for keeping it stabled. With the use of common sense and knowledgeable horsemastership it is of course possible to keep a horse at grass fit enough not only for ordinary Riding Club activities, but also for the competitions, but the fact remains that for various reasons ponies are better adapted than horses to living out.

Whether one rides a horse or a pony is of no consequence until it comes to the annual competitions for the Championships when animals of 14.2 and under are precluded, which is a pity. Apart from considerations of convenience and cost, there are many riders who would like to have a go at their Riding Club competitions, but who cannot do so unless they sell the much loved and well schooled pony of their youth in order to buy a more expensive horse of unknown potential. Obviously the fences in a competition including jumping will

Left, happy children and excited ponies off to a rally of Pony Club games.

Below, 'Never seen one like this before, for once I've actually got to land on a fence' . . . A competitor tackles the bank at the Pony Club Horse Trials Championships.

be constructed with the horses' scope and stride in mind, but a good pony is usually capable of coping, and does not have to be an out-of-this-world performer like the incomparable Stroller to do so!

Many of the Riding Club competitions are the same as those of the Pony Club, but at a different standard. There are Championships for Dressage, Show Jumping and The Riding Club Horse Trials, all run off first at area level. The finals of the Dressage, Horse Trials and the novice dressage-cum-riding test known as the Prix Caprilli, all take place each autumn at a special Riding Clubs' Weekend, held at the National Equestrian Centre.

As well as the competitions there are various Riding Clubs' tests to be acquired, and a special series of awards devised especially for riders whose riding time and area is particularly restricted. The scheme is non-competitive but the awards become progressively more difficult, and they test ability in horsemanship with a knowledge of farming, forestry and lore of the countryside.

All the Riding Clubs' competitions and championships carry some reservations about the previous successes and experience of both riders and horses, and animals under five are barred, except in the Prix Caprilli where four-year-olds are eligible. In the official events each horse or pony must either belong to the member, or to the Club concerned, or to a riding school where it has been regularly ridden by members of the Club for at least three months.

Pony Clubs and Riding Clubs did much after both World Wars to encourage and aid the transition of horses from being a necessary part of everyday life to becoming a general source of pleasure to a great many people. Not only did they fill the gap in a modern generation's knowledge of horse care and riding, they also provoked increasingly wide interest in a competitive age by the institution of competitions, events, horse trials, trekking and tests. Riding is now everywhere on the increase and Pony Clubs' and Riding Clubs' memberships and the number of shows grow larger each year.

Below, a riding party near Canberra, Australia.

Right. 'Life's very exhausting when you're only very young . . .'

Acknowledgements

The publishers would like to thank the following individuals and organizations for their kind permission to reproduce the pictures in this book:

Ackermann 86, 88.
American Paint Horse Association 28.
Associated Freelance Artists Ltd 12 bottom.
Australian News & Information Bureau 74, 75, 76, 129, 134.
Austrian National Tourist Office 67.
Barnaby's Picture Library 16, 18, 19 bottom, 20–21, 33, 34, 37, 49, 57, 68, 69, 78 bottom, 128.
British Percheron Horse Society 82 bottom.
Camera Press endpapers, 38, 46, 65, 66, 80.
Judith Campbell 15, 23, 25, 47, 120, 121, 126.
Colour Library International 11, 12 top, 78 top right, 127.
Rex Coleman 61 top.
Courtauld Institute of Art 89 bottom.
Department of the Environment 6.
Hartley Edwards 131.
Mary Evans Picture Library 8, 13, 14, 26, 27.
Charles Fennell 55.
Florida News Bureau 110.
Fores Ltd London 86, 88.
Fox Photos Ltd 43.
J. Hardman 45
Clive Hiles 133.
Michael Holford 10, 30.
Dan Hubbell 32 centre.

John F Hughes 58.
Keeneland Library 104.
Keystone Press Agency 60.
E D Lacey 50, 61 bottom, 62, 63, 92.
Leslie Lane 35, 44, 45, 52, 53 top, 70, 71, 73, 82 top, 83, 132.
M B Linney 22, 81.
Colin Lofting 32.
London Express News & Feature Service 95 bottom.
Mansell Collection 103.
New York Racing Association 99, 102, 104, 109, 112, 114–115.
Octopus Books 95 top.
Walter D Osborne 105, 106, 107, 108.
M. A. Owen 39.
Press Association 91.
Picturepoint 59 top.
Peter Roberts 123, 124.
W W Rouch & Co Ltd 89 top.
Alec Russel 117.
'Saddle & Bridle', Missouri 29 bottom.
Spectrum title page, 9, 20–21 top, 42 top, 53 bottom, 84, 96, 119, 122, 125, 130, 135.
Sport & General Press Agency 87, 90, 93, 94, 96 centre, 97, 98, 116.
'Stud & Stable' 113.
Peter Sweetman 54.
Sally Anne Thompson 41, 42 bottom, 59 bottom, 60, 77, 79.
United States Trotting Association 78 top left.
United States Fish & Wildlife Service 36.
'Voice of Tennessee Walking Horse' 29 top.
Barbara Woodhouse 51, 56.